JN086584

Furigana
JAPAN

Long-ago Stories
of Japan

Carla Valentine = translator

日本昔ばなし

カルラ・ヴァレンタイン＝訳

IBC

Furigana JAPAN

日本昔ばなし
Long-ago Stories of Japan

© 2021 IBC Publishing, Inc.

Published by IBC Publishing, Inc.
Ryoshu Kagurazaka Bldg. 9F, 29-3 Nakazato-cho
Shinjuku-ku, Tokyo 162-0804, Japan

www.ibcpub.co.jp

First edition 2021

ISBN978-4-7946-0656-3

Printed in Japan

About *Furigana JAPAN*

Reading Sets You Free

The difficulty of reading Japanese is perhaps the greatest obstacle to the speedy mastery of the language. A highly motivated English speaker who wants to make rapid progress in a major European language such as Spanish, French or German need only acquire a grasp of the grammar and a smattering of vocabulary to become able to at least attempt to read a book. Thanks to a common alphabet, they can instantly identify every word on the page, locate them in a dictionary, and figure out—more or less—what is going on.

With Japanese, however, *kanji* ideograms make it infinitely harder to make the jump from reading with guidance from a teacher to reading freely by oneself. The chasm dividing the short example sentences of textbooks from the more intellectually rewarding world of real-world books and articles can appear unbridgeable. Japanese—to borrow Nassim Taleb's phrase—is an "Extremistan" language. *Either* you master two thousand *kanji* characters with their various readings to achieve breakthrough reading proficiency and the capacity for self-study *or* you fail to memorize enough *kanji*, your morale collapses, and you retire, tired of floating in a limbo of semi-literacy. At a certain point, Japanese is all or nothing, win or lose, put up or shut up.

The benefits of staying the course and acquiring the ability to read independently are, of course, enormous.

Firstly, acquiring the ability to study by yourself without needing a teacher increases the absolute number of hours that you can study from "classroom time only" to "as long as you want." If there is any truth to the theories about 10,000 hours of practise being needed to master any skill, then clearly the ability to log more hours of Japanese self-study has got to be a major competitive advantage.

Secondly, exposure to longer texts means that your Japanese

input rises in simple quantitative terms. More Japanese *going into* your head means that, necessarily, more Japanese *stays in* your head! As well as retaining more words and idioms, you will also start to develop greater mental stamina. You will get accustomed to digesting Japanese in real-life "adult" portions rather than the child-sized portions you were used to in the classroom.

Thirdly, reading will help you develop tolerance for complexity as you start using context to help you figure things out for yourself. When reading a book, the process goes something like this: You read a sentence; should you fail to understand it first time, you read it again. Should it still not make sense to you, you can go onto the next sentence and use the meaning of that one to "reverse-engineer" the meaning of its predecessor, and so on. By doing this, you will become self-reliant, pragmatic and—this is significant—able to put up with gaps in your understanding without panicking, because you know they are only temporary. You will morph into a woodsman of language, able to live off the land, however it may be.

That is the main purpose of *Furigana JAPAN*: to propel you across the chasm that separates those who read Japanese from those who cannot.

Furigana the Equalizer

Bilingual books have been popular in Japan since the 1990s. Over time, they have grown more sophisticated, adding features like comprehensive page-by-page glossaries, illustrations and online audio. What makes the *Furigana JAPAN* series—a relative latecomer to the scene—special?

The clue is in the name. This is the first ever series of bilingual books to include *furigana* superscript above every single *kanji* word in the text. Commonly used in children's books in Japan, *furigana* is a tried-and-tested, non-intrusive and efficient way to learn to read *kanji* ideograms. By enabling you to decipher every word immediately, *furigana* helps you grasp the meaning of whole passages faster without needing to get bogged down in fruitless and demoralizing searches for the pronunciation of individual words.

By providing you with the pronunciation, *furigana* also enables you to commit new words to memory right away (since we remember more by sound than by appearance), as well as giving you the wherewithal to look them up, should you want to go beyond the single usage example on the facing English page. *Furigana JAPAN* provides a mini-glossary at the foot of each page to help you identify and commit to memory the most important words and phrases.

Raw Materials for Conversation

So much for *furigana*—now for the "Japan" part of the name. The books in this series are all about Japan, from its customs, traditions and cuisine to its history, politics and economy. Providing essential insights into what makes the Japanese and their society tick, every book can help you as you transition from ignorant outsider to informed insider. The information the books contain gives you a treasure trove of raw materials you can use in conversations with Japanese people. Whether you want to amaze your interlocutors with your knowledge of Japanese religion, impress your work colleagues with your mastery of party-seating etiquette and correct bowing angles, or enjoy a heated discussion of the relative merits of arranged marriages versus love marriages, *Furigana JAPAN* is very much the gift that keeps on giving.

We are confident that this series will help everyone—from students to businesspeople and diplomats to tourists—start reading Japanese painlessly while also learning about Japanese culture. Enjoy!

Tom Christian
Editor-in-Chief
Furigana JAPAN Series

まえがき

　世界中どの国や地方にも民話や童話があります。

　人類のルーツを調べる上で、似かよった童話を探してゆくことはとても大切なことだといわれています。

　しかし、実は今我々が子供に話して聞かせている童話は決して太古からあった童話であるとはいえません。

　童話は、歴史の中で子供をどのように教育するべきかという、その時その時の為政者の影響を強く受け、物語自体が創作されてきたのです。

　質素や倹約、あるいは謙虚さで人との和を大切にすべきという儒教道徳の影響や、因果応報という仏教的な影響が日本の童話には混在しています。童話は、単に子供に面白い話をするためにつくられたのではなく、子供を教育する目的を持って語られてきたのです。ですから、童話を読めば、その国の文化背景や人々の価値観を読みとることができるのです。

　また、童話は時には為政者に直裁に利用され脚色されます。「桃太郎」のように、大和朝廷が他の部族を平定してゆく過程のなかで、敵を「鬼」と設定した例などはその典型であるといえましょう。そして、「桃太郎」は、明治時代に再び脚色され、日本がアジアに進出するときに、桃太郎を正義の味方である日本人に、鬼を悪い敵になぞらえて語られてゆきました。

Preface

Every country and region of the world has folklore and fairytales.

It is said that when researching the roots of humankind, it is very important to look for fairytales with similarities in them.

However, it certainly cannot be said that the fairytales we actually tell to our children today are ancient ones. That is because throughout history, the fairytales themselves have been created with strong influences from people in power at that time to show how children should be educated.

The influence of Confucianism's ethic of placing importance on harmonious relations with other people through frugality, thrift, or modesty is mixed with the Buddhist influence of karma, in Japanese fairytales. Fairytales are not just made to be interesting stories for children; they are stories that are told to educate them. For this reason, when you read fairytales, you can understand a country's cultural background and people's values.

Fairytales are often used and modified as propaganda for people in power at that time. It can be said that the process by which the Yamato Court subjugated clans in each area and made the enemies into "ogres" in stories like "Momotaro" is a typical example of this type of thing. "Momotaro" was also dramatized again in the Meiji period, and when Japan invaded Asia, the story was told with Momotaro being linked to Japanese people as a hero of justice, and the ogres to evil enemies.

童話にも、こうした歴史の陰があることを知っておくべきかもしれません。

　とはいえ、日本人に様々な影響を与え、我々にとっても懐かしい童話の数々を英語で語ることは素敵な試みです。アメリカのように、様々な国からの人が集まって生活しているところでは、それぞれの人のルーツや文化を語りあうために、教育の場でよく出身国の童話などが紹介されます。

　海外に行き、交流するときに、向こうの子供に英語で日本の童話を語ってあげることは、相手の人からも喜ばれるに違いありません。

　ぜひ、本書で、昔の記憶を呼びおこし、思いだした童話をさらに英語で語る練習をしてみてはいかがでしょうか。

IBCパブリッシング編集部

It is probably a good idea to keep in mind that this kind of history is hidden in fairytales as well.

Anyway, these stories have influenced Japanese people in many ways, and it can be fantastic to try telling the stories that make us feel so nostalgic in English. Like in America, where there are people from various countries living together, in order to talk together about the roots and cultures of various peoples, fairytales from people's countries of origin are often introduced in educational settings.

When you go abroad and interact with foreigners, telling the children Japanese fairytales in English will definitely make the listeners happy too.

By all means, please wake up your memories of the past with this book and also practice trying to tell the fairytales you have remembered in English.

IBC Publishing

目<ruby>次<rt>じ</rt></ruby>

Contents

桃太郎

Momotaro

昔々、あるところに、おじいさんとおばあさんが住んでおりました。二人の家は、山と川とにはさまれたところにありました。毎日、おじいさんは山に薪をとりに、おばあさんは川に洗濯に行っておりました。

　ある日のこと、いつものようにおばあさんは川へとおりていきました。そして、洗濯をおえて顔をあげると、大きな桃が見えるではありませんか。桃は水の中で、浮いたり回ったり。重そうで丸くて桃いろ。とてもおいしそうです。でも、おばあさんは桃に手が届きません。

　「おいで。おいで。こっちじゃよ」おばあさんは呼んでいます。「こっちの水は甘いよ！」

14

Long, long ago somewhere, there lived an old man and woman. The old couple's house stood between a mountain and a river. Each day, the old man went up the mountain to cut wood, and the old woman went down to the river to wash clothes.

One day, as always, the old woman was down at the river. When she finished the wash, she looked up and saw a great big peach. The peach was bobbing and rolling in the water. It was heavy and round and pink, and it looked delicious. But it was just out of reach.

"Come over here!" the old woman called out. "The water's sweeter over here!"

□ 昔々 Long, long ago
□ あるところ somewhere
□ 山と川にはさまれた between a mountain and a river
□ 薪 *firewood*

□ ある日のこと one day
□ いつものように as always
□ おいしそう look delicious
□ 手が届かない out of reach

するとなんと大きな桃は、おばあさんの方に動きはじめるではありませんか。それは、浮いたり回ったり。回ったり浮いたり。そしておばあさんの腕のところにまっすぐやってきたのです。おばあさんは、桃を水から引きあげて、にっこり。早くこのすてきな桃をおじいさんと食べたいなと思いました。

日も暮れたころ、おじいさんは薪を背おって家にもどってきました。おばあさんが桃を見せるとおじいさんはびっくり。桃を両手で持ちあげて言いました。

「なんて大きな桃じゃろう。新しいうちに食べてしまおう」

おじいさんは桃を食卓において包丁を持ってきました。すると、桃が動きはじめるではありませんか。

「なんじゃ。なんじゃ」おばあさんが言いました。

「これは生きておるぞ」おじいさんは叫びました。

すると、桃がいきなり二つに裂けて、元気な男の赤ちゃんが飛びだしてきたのです。

「わーーーん」赤ちゃんは太鼓のような大きな声で泣いています。

おじいさんとおばあさんは、もちろんびっくり仰天。でも、とってもうれしい！

「いつもいつも、子どもを授けてくださいとお祈りしていたからねえ」おばあさんはそう言いました。

「神さまがくだされたのじゃ。さあ産湯がいるぞ」

And, sure enough, the great peach began to move toward her. It bobbed and rolled and rolled and bobbed, straight into her arms. The old woman pulled the peach out of the water and smiled. She couldn't wait to share this wonderful fruit with her husband.

That evening, as always, the old man came home with a load of wood on his back. When his wife showed him the peach, he couldn't believe his eyes. He picked it up and held it in both hands.

"Look at the size of it!" he said. "Let's eat it while it's fresh!"

He placed the peach on the table and picked up a knife. But just then the peach began to move.

"What's happening?" said the old woman.

"It's alive!" her husband shouted.

Suddenly the peach broke in two, and a healthy baby boy jumped out!

"WAAAAAH!" cried the baby, with a voice as loud as a drum.

The old man and woman were, of course, very surprised. But they were also very happy.

"We always prayed for a child of our own!" the old woman said.

"He's a gift from the gods!" said her husband. "Let's prepare his first bath!"

□ にっこり smile
□ びっくり can't believe one's eyes
□ 両手で in both hands
□ 食卓 table
□ 包丁 *kitchen knife*

□ なんじゃ（なんだ）What's happening?
□ 二つに裂ける break in two
□ びっくり仰天（する）be very surprised
□ 子どもを授かる *be blessed with children*
□ 産湯 first bath

おじいさんがそう言って、火をおこしてお湯を沸かしました。お湯をたらいにいれて、おばあさんが赤ちゃんをお湯にいれようとしたとき、赤ちゃんはそれをはねのけて、自分でお湯のなかに入ってゆきました。

「まあ、なんて力のある子なのじゃ」おじいさんとおばあさんは見つめあって大笑い。

「なんて名前にしましょうか」おばあさんがそう言うと、

「そうじゃな。桃から生まれたから、桃太郎としよう」とおじいさんは答えます。

*

おじいさんとおばあさんは桃太郎をとても大切に育て、桃太郎は元気な強い子に育ちました。小さい頃から、桃太郎は村いちばんの相撲とり。12歳になったときには、国じゅうの男たちの誰も、桃太郎を投げたおすことができなくなりました。それで、国じゅうの誰よりも桃太郎はやさしくて親切。

14歳になったときのことでした。桃太郎はおじいさんとおばあさんの前に座って、深くおじぎをします。

「おばあさん。そしておじいさん。しばらくお暇をいただきたいのです」桃太郎はそう言います。

「なんじゃと。どこに行こうというのじゃ」おばあさんはたずねます。

「鬼ヶ島に」

The old man made a fire and heated some water. When he filled the tub, his wife reached for the baby. But the baby pushed her away and climbed into the hot water all by himself.

"Such power!" the old couple laughed and looked at each other.

"What shall we name him?" the old woman said.

"Well, he was born from a peach," said the old man. "So let's call him Momotaro."

*

Thanks to the old couple's loving care, the "Peach Boy" grew up healthy and strong. Even when he was little, Momotaro was the best sumo wrestler in the village. By the time he was twelve, no man in all of Japan could throw him. And yet he was the sweetest, kindest boy in the land.

Momotaro was only fourteen when he went before the old man and woman and bowed deeply.

"Grandmother, Grandfather," he said. "I must leave you for a while."

"What?" said the old woman. "But where will you go?"

"To Demons Island."

□ 火をおこす make a fire
□ お湯を沸かす heat water
□ たらい tub
□ はねのける push away
□ 見つめあう look at each other

□ 名前にする name O
□ 深くおじぎをする bow deeply
□ お暇をいただく leave
□ 鬼ヶ島 Demons Island

「鬼ヶ島とや。何のために」おじいさんはびっくりして叫びました。

「鬼退治。そして宝物を持って帰ります」桃太郎はそう言いました。

その頃、鬼は人々のところにやってきては、金銀、そして宝石を無理矢理奪っていたのです。人々は皆、鬼のことをたいそう怖がっていました。

「鬼ヶ島は遠いぞ」おじいさんは言いました。

「それに、そんな危ないことを」おばあさんも言いました。

「ご心配なく」桃太郎は言いました。「すぐに宝を持ってもどってまいりますから」

おじいさんもおばあさんも、桃太郎が、鬼ヶ島に行くことはいやでした。しかし、桃太郎を止めることはできないと思いました。桃太郎は決して夢をあきらめないからです。そこで、おじいさんは桃太郎に剣とひとそろいの鎧をわたしました。そしておばあさんは、きびだんごをつくってくれました。きびだんごは、桃太郎の大好物だったのです。それにおばあさんは、桃太郎のために旗もつくってくれました。その旗には桃の絵と日本一という文字が描かれています。

「日本一の桃太郎」です。

＊

"Demons Island?" cried the old man. "Whatever for?"

"To fight the demons," said Momotaro, "and bring back all the treasure."

In those days, you see, demons often came to people. They pushed the people around and took away their gold and silver and jewels. Everyone was afraid of them.

"But Demons Island is so far!" said the old man.

"And so dangerous!" said the old woman.

"Please don't worry," said Momotaro. "I'll be home with the treasure in no time."

The old man and woman didn't want their boy to go, but they knew they couldn't stop him. Momotaro always followed his dreams. So the old man gave him a sword and a suit of armor, and the old woman made him some millet dumplings—his favorite food. She also made a flag for Momotaro to carry. On the flag was a picture of a peach and the words *Nippon Ichi*.

That means "Number One in Japan."

*

□ (いったい)何のために Whatever for?
□ 鬼退治 to fight the demons
□ その頃 in those days
□ 奪う take away
□ 夢をあきらめない follow one's dreams
□ 剣 sword
□ ひとそろいの鎧 a suit of armor
□ きびだんご millet dumpling
□ 大好物 one's favorite food
□ 日本一 Number One in Japan

桃太郎は、きびだんごをいれた包みを腰に巻いて、旗を高々と掲げ、旅にでます。やがて村から山に入ってゆきます。

山道をのぼってゆくと、犬が突然薮から出てきます。

「ワン！ワン！ 桃太郎、どこに行くの」

「鬼ヶ島に鬼退治」

「すごいね。包みに入っているものは？」

「日本一のきびだんご」

「一つおくれよ。ワン！ そしたら僕もついてくよ」

「ほら、お食べ。そして僕についといで」

＊

それから桃太郎と犬は森のなかを歩いてゆきます。すると突然お猿さんが木からおりてきます。

「キー！キー！ 桃太郎、どこに行くの」

「鬼ヶ島に鬼退治」

「すごいね。包みに入っているものは？」

「日本一のきびだんご」

「一つおくれよ。キー！ そしたら僕もついてくよ」

「ほら、お食べ。そして僕についといで」

＊

桃太郎と犬とお猿さんは広い野原を歩きます。すると突然雉が空から飛んできます。

「ギー！ギー！ 桃太郎、どこに行くの」

The Peach Boy tied the bag of millet dumplings to his belt, held the flag high, and set out on his journey. He soon left the village behind and started up the mountain.

Now he was climbing the mountain pass. Suddenly a dog came out of the brush.

"*Arf! Arf!* Where are you going, Momotaro?"

"To Demons Island, to fight the demons."

"Interesting! What's in the bag?"

"The best millet dumplings in all Japan."

"Give me one—*Arf!*—and I'll go with you!"

"Here you are, friend. Now follow me!"

*

Now Momotaro and the dog were marching through a forest. Suddenly a monkey climbed down from a tree.

"*Key! Key!* Where are you going, Momotaro?"

"To Demons Island, to fight the demons."

"Interesting! What's in the bag?"

"The best millet dumplings in all Japan."

"Give me one—*Key!*—and I'll go with you!"

"Here you are, friend. Now follow me!"

*

Now Momotaro and the dog and monkey were marching across a wide green plain. Suddenly a pheasant flew down from the sky.

"*Whirr! Whirr!* Where are you going, Momotaro?"

☐ 包み bag
☐ 旅にでる set out on a journey
☐ 山道 mountain pass
☐ 薮 brush
☐ ほら、お食べ。 Here you are.

☐ 野原 green plain
☐ 雉 pheasant

「鬼ヶ島に鬼退治」

「すごいね。包みに入っているものは？」

「日本一のきびだんご」

「一つおくれよ。ギー！ そしたら僕もついてくよ」

「ほら、お食べ。そして僕についといで」

*

桃太郎と犬とお猿さん、そして雉は一緒に海辺へ歩いてゆきます。そこには立派な船がありました。

「よし、みんな、船に乗ろう！」桃太郎は号令します。「鬼ヶ島目ざして、出航だ！」

天気はよく、風もあり、船は矢のように速く青い海をわたってゆきます。犬は櫓をこぎ、お猿さんは舵をとり、そして雉は見はりをします。やがて雉が叫びます。

「ギー！ ギー！ 島が見えたぞ」

桃太郎は舳先に走って、鬼がつくった城の高く黒い城壁を見つけます。

「あれだ。真正面があの鬼ヶ島だ！」

犬はオールを漕いで、ワン！ ワン！ お猿さんは船をまっすぐ進めてキー！ キー！ そして雉は島を目指して飛びだします。

"To Demons Island, to fight the demons."

"Interesting! What's in the bag?"

"The best millet dumplings in all Japan."

"Give me one—*Whirr!*—and I'll go with you."

"Here you are, friend. Now follow me!"

*

Now Momotaro and the dog and monkey and pheasant were marching down to the sea. A fine ship was waiting there on the beach.

"All aboard!" said Momotaro. "We'll sail the ship to Demons Island!"

It was a fine day, with a good wind. The ship raced like an arrow across the deep blue sea. The dog was rowing, the monkey was steering, and the pheasant was standing watch. Before very long, the pheasant called out:

"*Whirr! Whirr!* I see an island!"

Momotaro ran to the bow. He could just make out the high black walls of Demons Castle.

"That's it!" he shouted. "Demons Island dead ahead!"

The dog pulled on the oar—*Arf! Arf!* The monkey held the ship steady—*Key! Key!* And the pheasant flew ahead to the island.

□ 立派な fine
□ 出航(する) sail the ship
□ 矢のように like an arrow
□ 櫓をこぐ row
□ 舵をとる steer
□ 見はりをする stand watch
□ 舳先 bow
□ 城壁 walls of a castle
□ 真正面 dead ahead
□ オールを漕ぐ pull on the oar

浜にいた鬼は雉を見つけることはできません。でも、船を見たのでびっくりして急ぎお城に逃げて、黒い門の鍵をかけます。船が、鬼ヶ島につくと、桃太郎と犬とお猿さんは船から飛びおり、お城に向かって進軍します。

　「門を開けるんだ！」犬はそう叫んで門をけります。「門を開けるか、さもなければ戦になるぞ」

　鬼は門を内側から押さえて開けません。すると雉がお城の塔から飛びおりてきて、鬼たちの目をつつきます。

　「痛い！　逃げるんだ」鬼は叫びます。

　さあ、お猿さんの出番です。お猿さんは壁をのぼって門を内側から開きます。

The demons on the beach didn't see the pheasant. But they saw the ship, and they were very afraid. They ran inside their castle and locked the big black gate. When the ship landed, Momotaro and the dog and monkey jumped out. They marched right up to the castle.

"Open up!" the dog shouted and kicked at the gate. "Open up, or prepare for war!"

The demons pushed against the gate from inside, to hold it closed. But the pheasant flew down from the castle tower and pecked at their eyes.

"It hurts!" the demons cried. "Run for your lives!"

Now it was the monkey's turn. He climbed over the wall and opened the gate from inside.

□ 浜 beach
□ 鍵をかける lock
□ ～に進軍する march right up to
□ 戦 war
□ 塔 tower

□ つつく peck
□ 逃げる run for one's life
□ 出番 one's turn

27

「桃太郎、ここに見参！」犬はそう言うと、桃太郎はお城の中に入ってゆきます。

＊

鬼の王さまが桃太郎たちに会いに出てきます。10人、あるいは12人の強そうな鬼を従えて。鬼は皆金棒を持っています。

「お前は何ものだ」鬼の王さまが口を開きます。

「僕は日本一の桃太郎。宝を返してもらいにやってきた」

「返してもらいたければ、戦ってからだ」鬼の王さまは金棒を振りあげます。

「お望みなら」桃太郎はそう言うと、戦いがはじまりました。

鬼たちは大きくて意地悪です。しかし、皆心は強くありません。雉が飛んできては、ギー！ ギー！ といって鬼たちの目をつつきます。犬は走ってくると、ワン！ ワン！ といって、鬼たちの足に嚙みつきます。そしてお猿さんは飛びかかりながら、キー！ キー！ といって、鬼の顔を引っかきます。すると鬼は金棒を投げだして泣きながら逃げてゆきます。

鬼の王さまだけが取りのこされました。王さまは前にでて、金棒で桃太郎をたたこうとします。すると桃太郎は飛びのくと、そのまま王さまを地面に投げとばします。そして、王さまの頭を強い腕で押さえつけます。

「やめてくれ！ 降参だ！」鬼の王さまは叫びます。「お前の勝ちだ。桃太郎。命だけは助けてくれ。宝は返すから」

"Momotaro of Japan!" the dog called out as the Peach Boy marched into the grounds.

*

The King of Demons stepped out of the castle to meet them. He had ten or twelve of his biggest, strongest demons with him. All of them carried iron clubs.

"Who do you think you are?" said the king.

"I'm Momotaro of Japan. And I've come to take back our treasure."

"Not without a fight, you won't!" The king held up his club.

"As you wish," said Momotaro, and the fight began.

Demons are big and mean, but they're weak of heart. The pheasant flew from one to another—*Whirr! Whirr!*—and pecked at their eyes. The dog ran from one to another—*Arf! Arf!*—and bit their legs. And the monkey jumped from one to another—*Key! Key!*—and scratched their faces. Before very long, the demons all threw down their clubs and ran away in tears.

The only one left was the king himself. He stepped forward and tried to hit Momotaro with his club. But Momotaro jumped out of the way and threw him to the ground. Then he locked the king's head in his powerful arm.

"Stop! I give up!" cried the king. "You win, Momotaro! Please don't kill me! You can have the treasure!"

□ ここに見参。 *Here comes someone.*
□ 〜を従えて ... with him
□ 金棒 iron club
□ お望みなら as you wish
□ 意地悪 mean
□ 噛みつく bite
□ 引っかく scratch
□ 取りのこされる (be) only one left
□ 飛びのく jump out of the way
□ 降参(する) give up

29

桃太郎はついに手をゆるめます。王さまは手をついて桃太郎に何度も感謝します。そして家来の鬼たちに、お城にある金銀財宝を荷車に積むように命令します。鬼たちはその荷車を船に積みこみます。

「二度とあなたの国の人々を苦しませません」そう鬼の王さまは誓ったのです。

「きっとだぞ」そう言うと、桃太郎は犬とお猿さんと雉といっしょに船に飛びのり、帰ってゆきます。

*

故郷では、おじいさんとおばあさんが桃太郎の帰りを待っていました。

「無事だといいのだが。いったいいつ帰ってくるのやら」おばあさんがそう言うと、

「おや！　帰ってきたぞ」とおじいさんが答えます。

桃太郎は丘から村へと行進してきていたのです。桃太郎のうしろには、金銀財宝がうず高く積まれた荷車を犬とお猿さんが引っぱっています。そのうえの青い空を雉が輪を描いて飛んでいます。

「おお我が子よ」おじいさんは叫びます。「お前ならやれると思っていたよ。桃太郎！」

「無事でなによりじゃ」おばあさんもそう言います。

皆大喜び、桜の花も満開でした。

Finally Momotaro let go. The king got down on all fours and thanked him again and again. Then he ordered his demons to fill a cart with all the gold and silver and jewels in the castle. They loaded the cart on the ship.

"We'll never bother your people again!" the King of Demons promised.

"See that you don't," said Momotaro. And he and the dog and monkey and pheasant jumped on the ship and sailed for home.

*

Back home, the old man and woman were waiting for their Peach Boy.

"I hope he's all right," the old woman said. "Oh, when will he return?"

"Look!" said the old man. "Here he comes now!"

Momotaro was marching down the hill toward the village. Behind him, the dog and monkey were pulling a cart full of gold and silver and jewels. Above the cart, in the clear blue sky, the pheasant flew in circles.

"That's our boy!" cried the old man. "We knew you could do it, Momotaro!"

"We're so glad you're safe!" the old woman said.

Everyone cheered, and the cherry trees were blooming.

□ 手をゆるめる let go
□ 手をつく get down on all fours
□ 金銀財宝 gold and silver and jewels
□ 荷車 cart
□ 積みこむ load

□ 苦しませる bother
□ 無事(である) be all right [safe]
□ 輪を描いて飛ぶ fly in circles
□ 大喜び cheer
□ 満開 bloom

A Sparrow with Her Tongue Cut Out

舌きり雀

昔々、ある村に、やさしいおじいさんと、いじわるなおばあさんが住んでいました。おじいさんは、雀が好きで、子どものようにかわいがっていました。でも、おばあさんは雀が大嫌いです。

　ある日のこと、雀が庭におりてきて、おばあさんが洗濯に使おうとしていた糊を食べてしまいました。おばあさんは、とても腹がたって、雀をつかまえると舌を切って、追いはらいました。雀は山に飛んでゆきます。

　やさしいおじいさんは、その話を聞いて、雀がとても可哀想になりました。そこで雀を見つけて、おばあさんのやったことを謝ろうと思いました。

　おじいさんは森に行って、人に、舌を切られた雀のお宿はとたずねます。そして、苦労してやっと雀のお宿を見つけました。

　「ここにお詫びにきたのだよ。大丈夫かい？　どうか許しておくれ」おじいさんは、そう言いました。

　「来てくれてありがとう。とても驚いたけど、あれは私が悪かったんです。どうか、ここで夕ご飯を食べていってください」雀がそう言うので、おじいさんは、雀のお宿に一晩泊まることにしました。

　次の日の朝、おじいさんが家に帰ろうとすると、雀が言います。「おじいさん、お土産がありますよ。大きいつづらと小さいつづら、どちらがお好き」

　「お土産なんて。でも、どうしてもと言うなら、小さい方をくださいな」

Long, long ago, there lived a kind old man and his mean old wife in a village. The old man loved sparrows and took care of them like his own children, but his wife hated them.

One day a sparrow flew to their garden and ate the starch while she was washing clothes. She got so angry that she caught the sparrow and cut her tongue out. Then she let it go. The sparrow flew toward the mountains.

The kind old man heard the story and felt very sorry for the sparrow. He decided to find her and say sorry to her for it.

As he was walking in the forest, he asked people, "Where is the house of the sparrow with its tongue cut out?" It was difficult, but he finally found the sparrow's house.

"I came here to say sorry to you. Are you all right? Please forgive us," he said.

"Thank you for coming here. I was shocked, but it was my fault. Why don't you eat some of our dinner?" said the sparrow. The old man stayed there that night.

Before he returned to his house next morning, the sparrow said to him, "These are presents for you. Which do you want, the big box or the small box?"

"I don't want either of them. But if I have to take one, I want the small one," said the man.

□ 雀 sparrow
□ 大嫌い(である) hate
□ 糊 starch
□ 舌 tongue
□ 可哀想になる feel sorry for

□ お宿 house
□ お詫び(を言う) say sorry
□ お土産 present
□ つづら box *(wicker clothes hamper)*

おじいさんは、つづらを背おって帰りました。そしてなかを見ると、たくさんのお金や金や銀、そして織物などが入っているではありませんか。

　それを見たおばあさんがおじいさんに言いました。「どうして大きなつづらをもらわなかったのかい。これから行ってとってこよう」

　おばあさんは森へ行くと、人に「舌を切られた雀のお宿はどこかいな」とたずねます。そして雀に会いました。

　「何しに来たの」雀はたずねます。

　「私はお前に会いたかったんだよ。あんなにいろいろと面倒をみたんだから」とおばあさんは言いました。

　「それならお入りなさい」雀はそう言います。

　するとおばあさんは、「わしもお土産がほしいのじゃ。大きなつづらがの」

　おばあさんは、大きくて重いつづらを背中に背おって、雀の宿をあとにします。

　家に帰る途中、おばあさんは一刻もはやくつづらの中が見たくて仕方がありません。そこで、道の上につづらをおろすと、それを開けてみたのです。驚いたことに、蛇やお化け、そしてムカデなどなど、怖いものが次から次へと出てくるではありませんか。おばあさんは気を失ってしまったということです。

He came home with a box on his back. He opened it to find a lot of money, gold, silver, clothes and so on in it.

The old woman asked him, "Why didn't you take the big one? I will go and get it."

As she was walking in the forest, she asked people, "Where is the house of the sparrow with her tongue cut out?" She met the sparrow.

"Why did you come here?" asked the sparrow.

"I wanted to see you because I took such good care of you," answered the old woman.

The sparrow said, "OK. Come in, please."

The old woman said, "I want a present, too. I want a big box."

She left the sparrow's house carrying the big, heavy box on her back.

On her way home, she couldn't help looking inside the box. She put it down on the road and opened it. To her surprise, snakes, ghosts, centipedes, other terrible things came out of the box one after another. She fainted.

□ 背おう on one's back
□ 織物 clothes
□ いろいろと面倒をみる take good care of
□ あとにする leave
□ 一刻もはやく *as soon as possible*

□ 〜したくて仕方がない can't help doing
□ 驚いたことに to one's surprise
□ ムカデ centipede
□ 次から次へと one after another
□ 気を失う faint

Monkey vs. Crab

さるかにがっせん
猿蟹合戦

昔々、ある村に蟹が住んでいました。ある日、蟹は、道におにぎりが落ちているのを見つけました。家に帰っていると、猿が声をかけてくるではありませんか。猿は、柿の種をもっていて、おにぎりがほしいので、蟹にそれをおくれと頼みました。そして蟹はお返しに柿の種をもらったのです。

　やがて、蟹は柿の種を庭に植えて、何年も毎日水をやりました。それは大きな木になって、たくさんの柿の実をつけたのです。

　そこに猿がやってきて、木にのぼって、柿をすべて食べてしまいました。そして、ひどいことに、柿の実を力いっぱい蟹に向かって投げつけたので、蟹は死んでしまいました。

　蟹が殺されたことを知った蟹の子どもたちはとても怒ります。そこで友だちの臼と蜂、そして針と栗に加勢を頼みます。猿が外に出ているあいだ、皆は猿の家に隠れて、猿が帰ってくるのを待ちました。

　やがて、猿は家にもどってきました。そしていろりの前に座って体を温めようとします。そこに焼けた栗が飛びだして、猿のお尻を焼いてしまいます。

Long, long ago, there was a crab living in a village. One day she found a rice ball on the road. On her way home she heard a monkey call her name. He had found a persimmon seed. He wanted to eat the rice ball, so he told her that she had to give him the rice ball. She did, and he gave her the seed.

Later, she planted it in her garden and gave it water every day for several years. It became a big tree with a lot of fruit.

The monkey came and climbed the tree. He ate up all the fruit. He was so mean that he threw the fruit at her as hard as he could and killed her.

Now her young crabs were very angry because the monkey had killed her. They asked their friends, a mortar, a bee, a needle and a chestnut to help them. While he was out, they hid in each part of the monkey's house and waited for him to come home.

Soon the monkey returned and sat in front of the cooking fire to warm himself. The hot chestnut jumped out and burned his bum.

□ 蟹 crab
□ おにぎり rice ball
□ 柿の種 persimmon seed
□ 臼 mortar
□ 針 needle

□ 栗 chestnut
□ 加勢を頼む ask someone to help
□ いろり cooking fire
□ 体を温める warm oneself
□ お尻 bum

猿は痛いよと叫びながら、薬箱に飛んでいって、それを開けました。しかし、そこで蜂が出てきて、猿の肩のところを針で刺します。

　猿は痛いよと叫びながら、水の入ったバケツまで走ってゆきました。しかし、そこで子どもの蟹が出てきて猿の体をのぼると、ハサミで毛や皮や耳を切りおとしてしまいます。

　猿はまた痛いよと叫ぶと、戸へと走って、家から飛びだします。そこに、屋根から大きな臼が飛びおりて、猿を殺してしまいましたとさ。

The monkey shouted with pain and ran to a medicine box and opened it, but the bee came out and stung him in the shoulder.

The monkey shouted with pain again and ran to the water bucket, but the young crabs came out from under it and climbed up his body. They pulled his hair, skin and ears with their hands.

The monkey shouted in pain one more time and rushed out of the door of the house. The big mortar jumped off the roof and killed him.

□ 薬箱 medicine box
□ 刺す sting
□ バケツ bucket
□ 飛びだす rush out
□ 飛びおりる jump off

□ （〜して）しまいましたとさ。 *That's what I heard.*

The Crane Gives Back

つる　　おんがえ
鶴の恩返し

昔々のこと、貧しい若者が山間の小さな家に住んでいました。両親とは死に別れ、一人寂しく暮らしていました。毎日若者は森へ行って木をあつめ、それを近くの町で売ってはなんとか生活をしていました。

　それは冬の初めの朝のこと。若者は雪ふる森を歩いていると、変な物音がするではありませんか。それは誰かが痛がっているような声です。音のする方に歩いてゆくと、そこにはきれいな白い鶴が雪の上に横たわっています。そして羽には矢が刺さっていたのです。

　「ああ、かわいそうに。誰がこんなことを」若者はそう言うと、鶴を腕に抱きかかえ、ゆっくりと矢を抜いてやりました。そして羽の傷を洗って、雪の中にもどしてやると、ゆっくりと鶴のもとを離れます。すると、鶴は羽を広げて、飛びたちます。そして、鶴は若者のうえで輪を描き、鳴くと、そのまま雲のなかに消えていきました。

　夜遅く、若者は家で火のそばに座っていました。天気はとても悪く、空には白い雪が舞い、強い風も吹いています。

*

Once upon a time, a poor young man lived in a little house in the mountains. His parents were both dead now, and the young man was very lonely. Each day he walked through the forest and collected wood. He sold the wood in the nearest town, and made just enough money to get by.

It was a morning in early winter. The young man was walking through the snowy woods, when he heard something strange. It sounded like a cry of pain. He followed the sound until he discovered a beautiful white crane. She was lying in the snow, with an arrow through her wing.

"You poor thing!" the young man said. "Who did this to you?"

He held the crane in his arms and gently pulled the arrow out. Then he cleaned her wing, set her down in the snow, and stepped back. The crane spread her wings and rose up into the air. She circled above the young man once, cried out, and flew off into the clouds.

Late that night, the young man was sitting by his fire at home. Outside, the weather was very bad. The sky was white with snow, and a strong wind was blowing.

*

□ 昔々のこと Once upon a time
□ 山間の in the mountain
□ 寂しい be lonely
□ なんとか生活をする make just enough money

□ 雪ふる森 snowy woods
□ 鶴 crane
□ 飛びたつ rise up into the air
□ 輪を描く circle

すると、誰かが戸を叩いています。若者は戸を開けてびっくり。とても美しい女の人がそこに立っているではありませんか。

「道に迷ってしまいました。一晩泊めていただけませんでしょうか」

「どうぞどうぞ」若者はそう言うと女の人を招きいれ、火の側に座らせて、あったかいお汁を持ってきました。

「ありがとうございます。本当にご親切に」女の人はお礼を言います。

「どうか気になさらずに、好きなだけここにいてください」若者はそう応えます。

Suddenly there was a knock at the door. When the young man opened it, he was very surprised. A beautiful young woman was standing on the front step.

"I have lost my way," she said. "May I spend the night here?"

"Of course!" said the young man. He invited her in, gave her a seat by the fire, and served her some hot soup.

"Thank you so much," she said. "You're very kind."

"You're most welcome," he told her. "Please stay as long as you like."

□ 戸を叩く knock at the door
□ 道に迷う lose one's way
□ 一晩泊まる spend a night
□ 招きいれる invite in
□ お汁 soup

□ どうか気になさらずに You're most welcome.
□ 好きなだけ as long as one like

実は、その後も天気はなかなかよくならず、女の人は何日もそこに滞在したのです。女の人は掃除や料理を手つだいます。若者にとって、その女の人と一緒にいるのは、とても楽しいことです。いなくなったらどんなに寂しいだろうと何度も思います。しかし、ある朝女の人がやってきて、「私を嫁にしてください」と言ったのです。

　若者は顔を真っ赤にして、

「私は貧しく、あなたを幸せにはできません」

と言いました。

「貧しさなんてどうでもいいんです。一緒にいられれば」

　そして二人は一緒になりました。

＊

In fact the bad weather continued, and the woman stayed for many days. She helped with the cleaning and cooking, and she was very good company for the young man. He often thought how sad he would be when she left. But then, one morning, she came to him and said:

"Please take me as your wife."

The young man's face turned bright red.

"I'm a poor man," he said. "I can't give you a good life."

"I don't care if we're poor," she told him, "as long as we can be together."

And so they married.

*

□ 滞在する stay
□ 嫁にする take someone as one's wife
□ 真っ赤にして be turned bright red
□ 幸せにする give someone a good life

□ 一緒にいられれば as long as we can be together
□ 一緒になる marry

二人はとても幸せな夫婦でした。しかし、それはとても長く寒い冬でした。しかも正月がやってこようというのに、お金も食べ物もほとんどありません。ある日、若者は心配のあまり妻に言いました。

「食べていけないかもしれないな」

　妻は少し考えて、「たしか奥の部屋にはた織り機がありましたね」

「あるよ。あれは母親のものだった」若者はそう応えます。

「私はそれで着物を織ります」妻はそう言うと、

「でも一つだけ約束してほしいのです。私が織物をしているとき、決してなかを見ないでください。絶対に。お願いです」

　若者は不思議に思いましたが、約束します。妻は小部屋に移って戸を閉めます。そしてそれから三日間出てきません。その間、若者は妻の姿をまったく見ることはなく、しかしはた織りの音は昼に夜に響いてきます。

　三日目の夜、妻はやっと部屋から出てきました。とても弱々しく疲れています。しかし妻はにこっと笑って、三反の白い布地を若者に手わたしました。

They were very happy as man and wife. But it was a long, cold winter. Now New Year's was coming, and they had no money and very little food. One day, the young man told his wife that he was worried.

"How will we eat?" he said.

His wife thought for a while before speaking.

"There is an old loom in the little room in back," she said.

"Yes," he said. "It was my mother's."

"I want to use it to weave some cloth," she told him. "But you must promise me one thing. Never look into that room when I'm weaving. This is very important. Please promise."

The young man thought this strange, but he gave her his word. His wife went into the little room and closed the door. And there she stayed for the next three days. The young man didn't see her in all that time, but he heard the sound of the loom day and night.

On the third night, his wife finally stepped out of the room. She looked weak and tired. But she smiled as she handed him three rolls of white cloth.

□ 正月 New Year
□ 少し for a while
□ はた織り機 loom
□ 着物を織る weave cloth
□ 約束する give one's word

□ 昼に夜に day and night
□ 弱々しく look weak
□ 三反 three rolls (of cloth)

「これを町で売ってください」

とても美しい布地でした。月明かりのようにきめ細かく、そしてやわらかく。その翌日、若者は反物を町のお金持ちの家に持ってゆきました。そしてその夜、大きな袋を三つ、どれもお米をいっぱいつめて帰ってきたのです。

「大切な妻よ、本当にありがとう。これで今年の冬もこせよう。そしてお金持ちがもっとこの反物をほしがっている。できるだけ早くまた織っておくれ。とてもよいお金になるから」

それを聞いた妻は、しばらく無言で、そのあと悲しそうに笑みを浮かべます。

「お望みなら、今すぐに」と言って、奥にある小さな部屋の戸へと歩いてゆきます。「でも、忘れないで。反物を織っているあいだ、決してなかを見ないと……」

*

一晩中、そしてその翌日も、若者ははた織りの音を聞きました。しかし、今度の音は前とは違います。ゆっくりと、重々しく。若者は妻のことが気になりました。そして、夜遅く、若者は痛みに泣く声を聞いたのです。約束を守るべきか、それともと思いながら、若者は部屋を見ずにはいられませんでした。

"Please take this to town and sell it," she said.

It was very beautiful cloth—as fine and soft as the light of the moon. The next day, her husband carried the rolls straight to the house of the town's richest man. And that night he came home with three big bags full of rice.

"My dear wife!" he said. "Thanks to you, we'll get through the winter. And the rich man wants to buy more! Please weave more cloth as soon as you can! Think of the money we can get for it!"

His wife said nothing at first. But then she smiled sadly.

"Of course. I'll begin right away," she said and walked to the door of the little room in back. "But please remember. You must never look in when I'm weaving..."

*

All that night and all the next day, the young man heard the sound of the loom. But the sound was different this time. It was slower, and heavier. He began to worry about his wife. And then, late in the evening, he heard another sound, like a cry of pain. Promise or no promise, he had to look into the room.

□ 月明かり light of the moon
□ きめ細かい fine
□ 冬をこす get through the winter
□ 反物 *roll of cloth*
□ できるだけ早く as soon as one can

□ 重々しい heavy
□ 夜遅く late in the evening
□ 約束を守るべきか、それとも promise or no promise
□ ～せずにはいられない have to do

そして、部屋の戸を開けたとき、若者はびっくり。妻はそこにはいませんでした。はた織り機のまえに座っていたのは、白い鶴だったのです。鶴は病気になったように弱々しく、その体からは多くの羽がなくなっていました。鶴は若者を見あげると、悲しそうに鳴きました。そして若者の目のまえであの美しい妻にもどったのです。

　若者は言葉も出ません。
　「お前は……お前は」

But what a shock he got when he opened the door! His wife wasn't there, but a white crane was sitting at the loom. The crane looked ill and weak, and many of her feathers were gone. When she looked up and saw the young man, she let out a sad cry. And then, right before his eyes, she turned back into his beautiful wife.

The young man couldn't even speak.

"You…" he said. "You're…"

□ 病気になったように look ill
□ 悲しそうに鳴く let out a sad cry
□ 目のまえで right before one's eyes
□ 言葉も出ない can't even speak

「そう」妻は言いました。「私は鶴です。あなたはあの日、私の命を助けてくれました。だから恩返しがしたかったのです。あなたを助けることで。だから、私は人になりました。そして、あなたの妻になれて、とても幸せでした。あなたを心からお慕いしていました。あなたが食べていくためにお金がいるというから、私は羽を折って反物を織りました。でもあなたはもっとお金がほしくなって……」

「大切な妻よ」若者はそう言うと泣きだしました。「私は知らなかった。もしわかっていれば……」

「私はあなたとずっと一緒にいたかった。でもあなたは私の秘密を知ってしまいました。それはあってはならないこと。私はここを去らなければなりません」

「いやだ！」若者は妻のあとを追って、玄関に行きます。「どうか、ここにいてくれないか。お金なんかどうでもいい。お前がいてくれればいいのだよ」

妻は外に出て、悲しげに振りかえります。

「お許しください。これはあってはならないことなのです」

すると、若者の目のまえで、妻は白い鶴になり、翼を広げて空に飛びたちます。

鶴は一度若者のうえをまわると、また悲しそうな声で鳴きました。そして、そのまま雲のなかへと飛んでゆき、二度と若者のまえに姿を見せることはありませんでした。

"Yes," said his wife. "I'm the crane. You saved my life that day, and I wanted to give back. I wanted to help you in return. So I became human...I was happy as your wife, and I learned to love you very much. When you said you needed money for food, I used my feathers to weave the cloth. But then you wanted *more* money..."

"My dear wife!" cried the young man. "I didn't know! If I—"

"My hope was to stay with you forever," his wife said. "But now that you know my secret, it is not to be. I must leave you."

"No!" The young man followed his wife to the front door. "Please don't leave! I don't need money! I only want you!"

His wife stepped outside and turned to look at him sadly.

"I'm sorry," she said. "It is not to be."

And then, right before his eyes, she turned back into a white crane.

The crane spread her wings and rose up into the air. She circled once in the sky above the young man and let out another sad cry. Then she flew off into the clouds, and he never saw her again.

□ 恩返し（をする）give back
□ 心からお慕いする love someone very much
□ それはあってはならないこと。 It is not to be.
□ 玄関 front door

The Mouse's Wedding

ねずみの嫁入り

これは、ねずみについての古いお話です。

昔々、あるところに、とてもかわいらしい若いねずみが住んでいました。そして、両親はいつも、「世界一すてきな男を娘のために見つけなければ」と言っていました。

ある日、お父さんはお母さんに言いました。「お母さんよ。太陽こそがもっともすてきだよ。だって、我々を照らして、明かりをくれるのだから」

二人は太陽のところに行って頼みました。「太陽さん。あなたは世界で最もすてきな男ですよね。どうか娘と結婚してくれませんか」

太陽は答えます。「うーむ。ねずみさん。私は世界で最もすてきな男じゃないよ。最もすてきなのは雲だよ。だって、雲はいつも私を遮るのだから」

「なるほど」お父さんはそう言うと、

二人で雲をたずねます。「雲さん。あなたは世界で最もすてきな男ですよね。どうか娘と結婚してくれませんか」

すると雲は言いました。「うーむ。ねずみさん。私は世界で最もすてきな男じゃないよ。最もすてきなのは風だよ。だって、風は私を吹き飛ばすのだから」

「なるほど」お父さんはそう言うと、

二人で風をたずねます。「風さん。あなたは世界で最もすてきな男ですよね。どうか娘と結婚してくれませんか」

This is an old story about a mouse.

Long, long ago there was a beautiful young mouse. The parents were always saying, "We must look for the most wonderful man in the world for our daughter."

One day the father said to his wife, "Mother, it is the sun that is the most wonderful, because it shines over us and gives us light."

They went to the sun and asked him, "Mr. Sun, you are the most wonderful man in the world, aren't you? Will you marry our daughter?"

The sun answered, "Well, Mr. Mouse, I am not the most wonderful man in the world. It is the cloud that is the most wonderful, because he covers me all the time."

"Oh, I see," said the father.

They went to the cloud and asked him, "Mr. Cloud, you are the most wonderful man in the world, aren't you? Will you marry our daughter?"

The cloud answered, "Well, Mr. Mouse, I am not the most wonderful man in the world. It is the wind that is the most wonderful, because he can blow me away."

"Oh, I see," said the father.

They went to the wind and asked him, "Mr. Wind, you are the most wonderful man in the world, aren't you? Will you marry our daughter?"

□ 娘 daughter
□ ～(し)なければ(ならない) must do
□ ～を照らす shine over
□ 遮る cover
□ なるほど。I see.

□ 吹き飛ばす blow away

63

すると風は答えます。「うーむ。ねずみさん。私は世界で最も
すてきな男じゃないよ。最もすてきなのは壁だよ。だって、壁は
私を止めることができるのだから」

　「なるほど」お父さんはそう言うと、

　二人で壁をたずねます。「壁さん。あなたは世界で最もすてき
な男ですよね。どうか娘と結婚してくれませんか」

　すると壁は答えます。「うーむ。ねずみさん。私は世界で最も
すてきな男じゃないよ。最もすてきなのはねずみだよ。だって、
ねずみは私をかじるのだから」

　「なるほど」お父さんはそう言うと、

　娘に近くに住んでいるすてきな若いねずみと結婚するように言
いました。

　「ああ、あなたは世界で最もすてきな男。どうか娘と結婚してく
ださいませんか」と二人は言いました。

　「よろこんで」若いねずみは言いました。

　お父さんもお母さんもとても満足。やがて二人にはたくさんの
孫ができたのでした。

The wind answered, "Well, Mr. Mouse, I am not the most wonderful man in the world. It is the wall that is the most wonderful, because he can stop me."

"Oh, I see," said the father.

They went to the wall and asked him, "Mr. Wall, you are the most wonderful man in the world, aren't you? Will you marry our daughter?"

The wall answered, "Well, Mr. Mouse, I am not the most wonderful man in the world. It is the mouse that is the most wonderful, because he can eat me."

"Oh, I see," said the father.

The parents decided to ask their daughter to marry a nice young mouse who lived near them.

"Oh, you are the most wonderful man in the world. Would you marry our daughter?" they said.

"I would be happy to," he said.

Both the father and his wife were very happy. Soon they had many grandchildren.

□ よろこんで(〜する) be happy to do
□ 孫 grandchildren

The Old Man with a Lump

こぶとりじいさん

昔々のこと、頬に大きなこぶのあるおじいさんがいました。ある日おじいさんは山に薪をとりに行きました。すると、いきなり雨が降りだしたので、おじいさんは山にある小さなお寺で雨やどり。

　おじいさんは、そこで眠ってしまいました。気がつくと、お寺の外でたくさんの赤鬼や青鬼が踊ったり、お酒をのんだりして騒いでいるではありませんか。おじいさんは踊りが大好き。一緒に踊りたくなってしまいました。

　おじいさんは鬼たちと一緒に踊っても怖くありません。鬼たちはおじいさんの踊りをとても気にいりました。

　朝がきて、鬼の頭が言いました。「おまえはとても踊りがじょうずだな。明日の夜もここに来い。それまでおまえの大切なこぶを預かっておいてやる」鬼は言いおわると、おじいさんのこぶを取ってしまったのです。

　おじいさんが家に帰っておばあさんにその話をしていると、隣のいじわるじいさんがそれを盗みぎきしたのです。

　いじわるじいさんにもこぶがありました。そこで、いじわるじいさんは、こぶを取られた正直じいさんよりも先にお寺に行って、鬼の来るのを待っていました。

Long, long ago there lived an old man who had a lump on his cheek. One day he went to a mountain to find firewood. It suddenly began to rain, so he went to a small temple on the mountain to stay dry.

He slept until he heard some music outside the temple. There were many red and blue demons dancing, drinking and enjoying themselves. He felt like dancing himself because he liked it very much.

He forgot to be afraid and joined the group of dancing demons. All the demons enjoyed his wonderful dancing.

When it became light in the morning, the leader of the demons said to him, "You are a wonderful dancer. You can come tomorrow night. Until that time, I will keep your important lump." The demon took his lump away.

When he returned home and told his old wife the story, the mean old man next door listened to what he said.

The mean old man had a lump, too, and that night he went to the temple before the nice old man and waited for the time to come.

□ 頬 cheek
□ こぶ lump
□ いきなり suddenly
□ 雨やどり（する）stay dry
□ 頭 leader

□ 預かる keep
□ 盗みぎきする *eavesdrop*

間もなく、たくさんの鬼が踊りをはじめました。いじわるじい
さんは、鬼が怖くてしかたありません。しかし、こぶを取っても
らいたいので、踊りはじめました。ところが、いじわるじいさん
の踊りと歌はとてもひどいものでした。
　鬼たちはとても怒って、正直じいさんのこぶをいじわるじいさ
んのもう片方の頬にくっつけたということです。

Soon many demons began to dance. He was very afraid of demons, but he wanted to have his lump taken away, so he started to dance. But his dancing and singing were very poor.

The demons got very angry and put the nice man's lump on his other cheek.

□ 間もなく soon
□ ひどい poor

Kachi Kachi Mountain

かちかち山

昔々、あるところに、年老いたお百姓のおじいさんとおばあさんが住んでいました。

　毎日、おじいさんは、畑に行きます。畑仕事は大変でした。ところが、裏山から狸がやってきて、おじいさんの仕事をもっと難しくしてしまいます。

　狸はアライグマと犬をかけ合わせたような動物で、昔から、いたずらをすることで知られています。この裏山の狸も毎日のように、おじいさんに意地悪をするのです。

　その日、お百姓のおじいさんは種を植えていました。

　「小さな種よ、たくさんの食べものになっておくれ」おじいさんは、一粒一粒種を土に入れるたびに、そう歌います。

*

　昼におじいさんは家でお昼ご飯を食べました。おじいさんがご飯を食べているあいだに、狸は畑にやってきて、種をすべて掘りおこし、食べてしまったのです。お百姓のおじいさんが仕事をしにもどってきたとき、狸を見つけ怒鳴りつけます。

　「この悪者め。ここから出てゆけ！」

　「たくさんの種が、ちょっとの食事」狸はそう言って笑うと、薮の中に走ってゆきました。

Long, long ago, an old farmer and his wife lived in a certain place.

Each day the farmer worked hard in his field. And each day a tanuki from the Mountain in Back made his work even harder.

A tanuki looks like a cross between a raccoon and a dog. This animal is famous in Japan for playing tricks on people. And the tanuki from the Mountain in Back was always causing trouble for the old farmer.

Today the farmer was planting.

"One little seed, a hundred meals!" he sang as he pushed each seed into the ground.

*

At noon he went inside the house for lunch. And while he was gone, the tanuki ran through the field, dug up all the seeds, and ate them. When the farmer came back outside, he saw the tanuki and shouted:

"You little devil! Get out of my field!"

"A hundred seeds, one little meal!" the tanuki laughed and ran off into the brush.

□ お百姓 farmer
□ 畑 field
□ 裏山 Mountain in Back
□ アライグマ raccoon
□ いたずらをする play a trick on

□ 掘りおこす dig up

おじいさんはとても腹がたちました。おじいさんは動物が好きですが、このやり方はあんまりです。おじいさんは午後をついやして、罠をつくります。

＊

　狸は、人にいろいろと迷惑をかけますが、あまり利口ではありません。その次の日の朝、お百姓のおじいさんが罠を見にゆくと、やっぱり。そこに狸がひっかかっているではありませんか。おじいさんは、狸の四本の足をしっかりと縄でくくり、家に運ぶと、縄の端を台所の梁にくくりつけます。

　「ついにこの悪い狸を捕まえた」おじいさんはおばあさんに言いました。「ちゃんと見はっていてくれよ。こいつのいたずらにひっかからないように。今夜は狸汁を食べようか」

　「そうしましょう」

　おばあさんは言いました。おじいさんが畑にもどってゆくと、おばあさんは家のまわりで仕事をはじめます。狸は何もしゃべりません。ただ、じっとおばあさんの動きを見ています。

　しばらくして、おばあさんは、台所にきてきびを臼にいれました。きび餅を狸汁に入れようと思ったのです。おばあさんが、きびを牽くために重い木づちを持ちあげたとき、狸はようやく口を開きます。

The farmer was very angry. He loved animals, but enough was enough. He spent the rest of the afternoon making a trap.

*

The tanuki was good at causing trouble, but he was not very bright. The next morning, the farmer went to check his trap. And, sure enough, there was the tanuki. He was hanging by all four feet at the end of a rope. The farmer carried him into the house and tied the other end of the rope to the kitchen rafters.

"I finally caught this bad tanuki," he told his wife. "Keep an eye on him, and don't fall for any of his tricks. I want tanuki soup for dinner!"

"Very well, dear," she said.

When the farmer went back out to his field, the old woman began working around the house. The tanuki didn't say a word. But his eyes followed her every move.

After a while, the old woman went into the kitchen and put some millet in the mortar. She wanted to make millet cakes to go with the tanuki soup. When she picked up the heavy wooden mallet, to pound the millet, the tanuki finally spoke.

□ あんまりだ enough is enough
□ ついやす spend
□ 罠 trap
□ 迷惑をかける cause trouble
□ 利口 bright

□ やっぱり sure enough
□ 梁 rafter
□ ～を見はる keep an eye on
□ きび餅 millet cake
□ 木づち wooden mallet

「おばあさん」その声は悲しそうです。「ごめんなさい。私は悪い狸でした。せめて死ぬ前に一つよい事がしたいのです。おばあさんの手つだいをさせてください。この木づちはあなたのようなお年よりにはとても重いはずですから」

「嘘をつくんじゃないよ」

おばあさんがそう言うと、「嘘なんか、つきません。おばあさん。私は喜んでおばあさんとおじいさんのために狸汁になりましょう。でも、この世を去るまえに一つだけ良いことがしたいのです」そう狸は懇願します。

おばあさんは心の優しい人でした。結局狸を信じてしまい、縄をほどいて重たい木づちを手わたします。しかし、狸は木づちを使っておばあさんを助けるどころか、なんとそれを高々と持ちあげて、おばあさんの頭の真うえから振りおろしたのです。

*

その日の午後おそく、おじいさんが家にもどってきました。おなかが空いていたので、狸汁を楽しみにして。ところがそこで見たものは……。なんとおばあさんが死んで、狸はどこかに行っているではありませんか。

"Grandmother," he said in a sad voice. "I'm sorry I've been such a bad tanuki. I want to do just one good thing before I die. Please let me help you. That mallet is much too heavy for an old woman like you!"

"You can't fool me," the old woman said.

"I'm not trying to fool you, Grandmother," the tanuki said. "I'm happy to be soup for you and the good farmer. But just once, before I leave this life, I want to do the right thing!"

The old woman had a soft heart, and in the end she believed the tanuki. She untied him and handed him the heavy wooden mallet. But he didn't use the mallet to help the old woman. He lifted it high in the air and brought it right down on her head!

*

Late that afternoon, the farmer came back home. He was hungry and looking forward to his tanuki soup. But what did he find? His dear wife was dead on the floor, and the tanuki was gone.

□ 嘘をつく *tell a lie*
□ 心の優しい have a soft heart
□ 結局 in the end
□ 高々と high in the air
□ 〜を楽しみにする look forward to

おじいさんは家の入りぐちに座りこみ、悲嘆にくれます。どう
していいかわかりません。おじいさんがそこに座りこんでいると、
かわいらしいうさぎが前の山からやってきました。うさぎはおじ
いさんの仲のいい友だちです。

　「どうしたの。おじいさん」うさぎはたずねます。
　お百姓さんは、ことのすべてをうさぎに話してきかせました。
涙が頬をつたって流れます。うさぎも一緒に泣きました。
　「ひどい狸ね！　心配しないでおじいさん、きっと敵はとってあ
げるからね」

＊

　次の日になりました。うさぎは裏山にのぼってゆきました。か
ごに薪をたくさん入れて。うさぎは狸の穴のそばに座って、栗を
食べながらひとやすみ。

　栗のにおいをかいで、狸は穴から出てきました。
　「うさぎ。お前何を食べている」狸はたずねます。
　「栗よ」
　「少し、おくれよ」
　「どうぞ」うさぎは応えます。「でも、その前に手つだって。こ
の薪を運んでくれない？　私にはとても重くて」

　「もちろん」

The old farmer sat down on the front step. His heart was broken, and he didn't know what to do. He was still sitting there, when the cute little rabbit from the Mountain in Front came along. This rabbit was a close friend.

"What's wrong, Grandfather?" she said.

The farmer told her the whole story. Tears were running down his face. The rabbit cried too.

"That terrible tanuki!" she said. "Don't worry, Grandfather. He won't get away with this!"

*

The next day, the rabbit walked up the Mountain in Back. As she walked, she filled her basket with pieces of wood. She sat down to rest near the tanuki's hole and began eating chestnuts.

The tanuki smelled the chestnuts and came outside.

"What are you eating, Rabbit?" he said.

"Chestnuts."

"Can I have some?"

"Yes," said the rabbit. "But please help me first. Can you carry this wood? It's so heavy for me…"

"Gladly!" said the tanuki.

□ 悲嘆にくれる one's heart broken
□ 仲のいい友だち close friend
□ どうしたの。 What's wrong?
□ ことのすべて whole story
□ 敵をとる *revenge*

□ 栗 chestnut
□ もちろん。 Gladly.

狸はそう言うと、薪の入ったかごを背中に担いで山をおりはじめます。うさぎはうしろからついてきます。そして、火打石を打ちはじめました。カチッ、カチッ！　うさぎはかごの薪に火をつけようとしているのです。

　「おいうさぎ。そのカチッ、カチッって音は何の音だ？」狸はききます。

　「別に。ただ、カチカチ山からきたカチカチ鳥がいるだけよ」

　「なるほど。俺さまもそんなことは知ってたよ」狸はそう言いました。

　やがて火打石の火の粉が薪に移り、薪は燃えてパチパチと音をたてます。

He tied the basket of wood to his back and started down the mountain. The rabbit followed behind him. Soon she began hitting two rocks together: *Kachi! Kachi!* She was trying to set the basket of wood on fire.

"Say, Rabbit," said the tanuki. "What's that 'kachi, kachi' sound?"

"Oh, that's nothing," said the rabbit. "It's just the Kachi Kachi Bird from Kachi Kachi Mountain."

"Oh, right," said the tanuki. "I already knew that."

Soon a spark from the rocks landed on the wood, and the wood started burning. It crackled as it burned.

□ うしろからついて follow behind
□ 火打石 *flint*
□ 別に。 That's nothing.
□ 火の粉 spark
□ パチパチと音を立てる crackle

「おいうさぎ。このパチパチって音は何の音だ？」

「別に。ただ、パチパチ山からきたパチパチ鳥がいるだけよ」

「なるほど。俺さまもそんなことは知ってたよ」

しばらくすると、狸の背中が熱くなります。

「おいうさぎ。いやに暑くないかい、今日は？」

誰もそれには応えません。

「おいうさぎ」

狸は振りかえりますが、うさぎはどこにもいませんでした。でもそこに火が。

「助けてくれ！」狸は叫びます。「燃えちゃうよ！」

狸はおお急ぎで川に向かって走りだします。

＊

さらにその次の日、うさぎは裏山にもどってきます。練った唐辛子をいっぱいかごに入れて。狸は穴から出て、うさぎを呼びとめます。

「昨日はどこに行ったんだ。うさぎ」狸は言います。「薪に火がついて、俺の背中の毛を焼いてしまった。痛いじゃないか」

「薬をとりに行ったのよ。やけどにきく薬をね」とうさぎは答えます。

「そうか。それを背中につけてくれ」狸はそう言いました。

「向こうを向いて」うさぎはそう言うと、狸のやけどのあとに、練った唐辛子をしっかりと塗りつけます。

"Say, Rabbit, what's that 'crackle, crackle' sound?"

"Oh, that's nothing. It's just the Crackle Crackle Bird from Crackle Crackle Mountain."

"Oh, right," said the tanuki. "I already knew that."

After a while, he began to feel the heat of the fire on his back.

"Say, Rabbit, it's hot today, isn't it?"

There was no answer.

"Rabbit?"

The tanuki turned to look back. He didn't see the rabbit, but he saw the fire.

"Help!" he shouted. "I'm burning!"

And he ran toward the river as fast as he could go.

*

The next day, the rabbit returned to the Mountain in Back. She was carrying a bag full of red hot pepper paste. The tanuki came out of his hole and stopped her.

"Where did you go yesterday, Rabbit?" he said. "The wood caught fire! It burned all the hair off my back! It hurts!"

"I went to get this medicine," said the rabbit. "It's the best thing for burns."

"Oh, please put it on my back!" said the tanuki.

"Turn around," the rabbit said. She painted a thick coat of pepper paste on the tanuki's burns.

□ おお急ぎで as fast as one can
□ 練った唐辛子 red hot pepper paste
□ やけど burn
□ 向こうを向いて。 Turn around.
□ しっかりと塗りつける paint a thick coat

「おー！　熱々！」狸は叫びます。

「我慢しなさい。明日にはよくなっているわ」うさぎはそう言うと、急いで山にもどります。

＊

そして、その次の朝、狸はうさぎが川におりてゆくのを見つけます。うさぎは木を使って舟をつくっていたのです。

「狸さん！　少しはよくなった？」

「ああ、まあね。でも昨日の夜はとても痛かった」

「それはよかったわ」

「何をやってるんだ」狸はたずねます。

「舟をつくってるの」

「なぜ」

「だって、川の真んなかで大きなお魚を捕まえたいの」

「そうか。俺も大きな魚がほしい。舟をつくっていいかい」

「もちろん」うさぎは応えます。「でもあなたは私より重いわね。泥で舟をつくらなきゃ」

「なるほど。俺さまもそんなことは知ってたよ」そう狸は言いました。

そして狸は川岸の泥をとって舟をつくります。それは大きなお椀のような舟でした。うさぎと狸は舟ができあがると、さっそく川の真んなかまで漕いでいきます。そこの水は冷たくて、とても深いのに、狸のどろ舟は、壊れはじめます。

"OH!" shouted the tanuki. "OH! THAT'S HOT!"

"Be strong," the rabbit said and smiled. "I'm sure you'll feel better tomorrow."

And she hurried back down the mountain.

*

The next morning, the tanuki found the rabbit down by the river. She was building a boat out of wood.

"Hello, Tanuki!" she said. "Do you feel better today?"

"I guess so," said the tanuki. "But last night I was in such pain!"

"That's good," said the rabbit.

"What are you doing?" the tanuki asked her.

"I'm building a boat."

"How come?"

"Well, I want to catch the big fish in the middle of the river."

"Oh! I want some big fish too! Can I build a boat?"

"Sure," said the rabbit. "But you're much heavier than I am. You should make your boat out of mud."

"Oh, right," said the tanuki. "I already knew that."

So the tanuki took mud from the bank of the river and made a boat. It was shaped like a big bowl. When both boats were finished, the rabbit and the tanuki rode them out to the middle of the river. The water was cold and deep there, and the tanuki's boat of mud began to fall to pieces.

□ 我慢しなさい。 Be strong.
□ なぜ How come?
□ 泥 mud
□ 川岸 bank of a river
□ お椀 bowl

□ 壊れる fall to pieces

「助けてくれ！」狸は叫びます。「うさぎ、助けて。俺は泳げないんだ！」

　しかし、うさぎは木でつくった舟をあやつって岸へと引き返すだけ。

　うさぎがお百姓のおじいさんの家に帰ってきたとき、すでに日も暮れかけていました。おじいさんは家の入りぐちに座っています。

　「あの狸はもう誰にも悪さはできないわ」

　おじいさんは何も言わず、手をうさぎの頭にのせました。そして一緒に太陽が沈んでいくのを見るのでした。

"Help!" he shouted. "Rabbit, save me! I can't swim!"

But the rabbit just turned her wood boat around and headed for land.

The sun was low in the sky when she got back to the old farmer's house. The farmer was sitting on the front step.

"That tanuki will never hurt anyone again," she told him.

The old man said nothing, but put his hand on the rabbit's head. And together they watched the sun go down.

□ 助けて。 Save me.
□ 舟をあやつる *operate a boat*
□ 太陽が沈んでいく the sun go down

The Bamboo Princess

かぐや姫

昔々、おじいさんとおばあさんがとある村に住んでいました。二人は竹を切って、籠やいろいろなものをつくって暮らしていました。

　ある日、おじいさんはいつものように森に行くと、輝く竹を見つけました。おじいさんがその竹を切ってなかを見ると、驚いたことに女の赤ちゃんがそこにいるではありませんか。

　おじいさんとおばあさんには子どもがいません。そこでその赤ちゃんを引き取ってかぐや姫と名づけました。それからというもの、おじいさんが竹を切るとそこにはいつも小判が入っています。やがて一家はお金持ちになりした。そしてかぐや姫は日を追うごとに育っていって、とても美しい娘になりました。その噂を聞いて、多くの男たちがあちこちからたずねてきて、かぐや姫をお嫁にもらおうとします。でも、かぐや姫は誰にも興味を示しません。

　かぐや姫はいつも何か他のことを考えているようで、ただ空を見つめています。

Long, long ago there lived an old man and his wife in a village. They cut bamboo and made baskets and other things out of it to get money.

One day the man went to the forest as always, and he found a shining bamboo plant. He cut it open, and to his surprise, he found a baby girl inside.

The old man and his wife had no children of their own, so they took her in and named her *Kaguya Hime* (Bamboo Princess). Every time the man went to cut bamboo after that, he found money in it. Soon he and his family became rich. Kaguya Hime grew day by day to be a very beautiful lady. Hearing of her beauty, many young men from various places visited her house because they wanted to marry her. But she never showed any interest in them.

She always looked like she was thinking about something else, and just looked up at the sky.

□ 竹 bamboo
□ 引き取る take in
□ 小判 money (*oval gold coin*)
□ 日を追うごとに day by day
□ あちこちから from various places

□ 何か他のこと something else

おじいさんは、**たびたびたずねてくる**男たちを**放っておくわけ**にもいきません。そこで、男たちに、この世で最もすてきな宝物を持ってきた者に、かぐや姫をお嫁にやると約束したのです。

何人かの男たちがとてもすてきな宝物を持ってきました。しかし、かぐや姫はそのどれにも満足ではありません。

やがて、かぐや姫は月を見る**たびに**泣くようになりました。

「どうしてそんなに悲しいのかい。**何があったのかね**」おじいさんはたずねました。

「**大丈夫です。私の話を聞いてください**。実は私は月で生まれたのです。そして**中秋の名月**のときに、**使いが迎えにきて**、月に帰らなければならないのです」

「なんということだ」おじいさんはびっくり。中秋の名月は明日ではありませんか。

おじいさんは、さむらいたちにお願いして、使者からかぐや姫を守ろうとします。かぐや姫が月に帰らないようにと心で祈りながら。

その夜、月が山から上ったとき、**いきなり**まぶしい明かりがおじいさんの家にいる男たちに降りそそぎます。さむらいたちは、月に向かって**矢を放ち**ました。しかし、何にもあたりません。そして、もっと明るく光ったとき、さむらいたちは、眠ってしまいました。

Her father could not ignore the men who were always visiting, so he told them that the man who brought the greatest treasure in the world would be able to marry her.

Some of the men brought wonderful treasures, but she always said that they were not special enough.

Soon she began to cry every time she saw the moon.

"What makes you so sad? What's the matter?" asked the father.

"I am all right. Listen to me. I was born on the moon. I must return to the moon on the night of the 15th of August, when some visitors are coming to pick me up."

"That is crazy," said the father. He was very angry. The 15th of August was the next day.

The father found a group of samurai to keep her safe from the visitors. He hoped that she would never return to the moon.

That night, as the moon was rising over the mountains, its light suddenly flashed down on the men at the old man's house. Many of them shot arrows at the moon, but none of them could hit it. Then, there was a bright flash of light, and they all began to sleep.

□ たびたび always
□ 放っておく ignore
□ (〜する)たびに every time
□ 何があったの。What's the matter?
□ 私の話を聞いてください。Listen to me.

□ 中秋の名月 the night of the 15th of August
□ 使い visitor
□ いきなり suddenly
□ 矢を放つ shoot arrows

月のお使いが、光に乗って、家におりてきます。かぐや姫は光に向かって動かずにはいられません。お使いに手をとられてゆっくりと空へとあがってゆきます。誰もそれを止めることはできませんでした。

　おじいさんも、おばあさんも、ただその様子を眺めているだけでした。

An angel came down through the light from the moon to the house. Kaguya Hime could not help moving toward the light. She slowly flew up to the sky hand-in-hand with the angel. Nothing could stop them.

The old man and his wife could do nothing as they watched her return to the moon.

□ お使い angel
□ 手をとられて hand-in-hand
□ ただ〜するだけ can do nothing (but) …

Grandfather Flowers

はな さ
花咲かじいさん

昔々、ある小さな村に、とても親切なおじいさんとおばあさん
が住んでいました。でも、そのお似合いの二人には残念なことに
子どもがいません。そんな二人は一匹の犬をとても大事にしてい
ました。白い犬だったので、シロと名づけられ、二人は自分の息
子のようにシロをかわいがっていました。

　ところで、その隣には、もう一組のおじいさんとおばあさんが
住んでいました。でもその二人はあまり良い人たちではありませ
ん。二人はよく張りで意地悪で、自分たちのことしか考えていま
せん。そして、二人はお隣が嫌いで、シロのことも嫌いでした。
かわいそうに、時々二人はシロに石を投げたりさえしていました。

　ある日、いつものように、親切なおじいさんは畑で仕事をして
いました。シロも、おじいさんといっしょ。地面に鍬をいれてい
るあいだ、シロは走りまわって、あちこちクンクンとにおいをか
いでまわります。突然、シロが畑の角にある大きな木のしたで止
まって吠えはじめました。

Long, long ago, a kind old man and woman lived in a little village somewhere. Sadly, these nice old people had no children. But they had a dog they loved very much. The dog was white, and his name was Shiro. Shiro was almost like a son to the kind old couple.

Now, another old man and woman lived next door. And this old man and woman were not so nice. In fact, they were greedy and mean. They cared only about themselves, and they didn't like their neighbors. They didn't like Shiro, either. Sometimes they even threw rocks at the poor dog.

One day, as always, the kind old man went out to work in his field. Shiro went with him. The old man turned the ground with his hoe, while Shiro ran around and enjoyed all the different smells. Suddenly Shiro stopped in one corner of the field, under a big tree, and started to bark.

□ とても大事にする love very much
□ 息子のように almost like a son
□ よく張り greedy
□ お隣 neighbor
□ ～さえ even

□ いつものように as always
□ 鍬 hoe
□ 吠える bark

「ここ掘れワンワン。ここだよ」

「どうしたシロ」

　親切なおじいさんはシロのまえの土を掘ってみます。すると鍬がなにか固いものにぶつかります。それは重い木の箱でした。なんと、驚いたことに、箱は小判でいっぱいでした。

　シロのおかげで、親切なおじいさんとおばあさんはお金持ちになりました。お隣のいじわるじいさんは、そのことが面白くありません。もちろんいじわるばあさんも同じです。

　「なんであんな愚かな年よりが良いめにあうのじゃ」いじわるばあさんはじいさんに言いました。「あの犬をさらっておいで、わしらにも宝を見つけてくれるに違いない」

"Hoe here! *Arf! Arf!* Hoe here!"

"What is it, Shiro?"

When the kind old man dug into the ground in front of Shiro, his hoe hit something hard. It was a heavy wooden box. And, to the old man's great surprise, the box was full of gold coins!

Thanks to Shiro, the kind old man and woman were now rich. When the mean old man next door heard about this, he was not happy. His wife wasn't happy either.

"Why should those old fools have all the luck?" she said to her husband. "Go get that dog! He can find some treasure for us too!"

□ 小判　gold coin
□ 〜のおかげで　thanks to
□ 愚かな　fool
□ 良いめにあう　have all the luck

「それはいい」いじわるじいさんは言いました。いじわるじい
さんは、隣に行って、シロの首に縄をつけて、かわいそうに、むり
やり自分の畑につれてゆきました。

「ここにも宝があるはずじゃ。探さんかい！」

縄はシロの首をしめるので、ついにシロは大声をあげて、倒れ
こみます。

「ここじゃな？」いじわるじいさんは、そこを掘って掘って、つ
いに柔らかい泥まで鍬をいれました。いじわるじいさんは、両手
でそれをすくいますが、そこには黄金はありません。そこにあっ
たのは泥とゴミ、そして小さな虫ども。ひどい臭いがしているで
はありませんか。

いじわるじいさんは、とても腹をたて、地団駄を踏んで、シロを
叱りつけます。そしてついに鍬を手にとりました。いじわるじい
さんは、鍬を振りあげて、思いきりシロの頭をたたいたのです。
かわいそうなシロは一哭きすると、死んでしまいました。

＊

"Good idea," said the mean old man. He marched right next door, tied a rope around Shiro's neck, and pulled the poor dog out to his field.

"There must be treasure here too," he said. "Find it!"

The rope hurt Shiro's neck, and finally he let out a cry and fell down.

"This is the place, is it?" the mean old man said and started digging. He dug and dug, and finally he broke through to soft mud. He reached in with both hands, but he didn't find any gold—just mud and waste and strange little bugs. A terrible smell filled the air.

The mean old man was very angry. He jumped up and down and shouted at Shiro, and finally he picked up his hoe. He lifted it over the poor dog's head and brought it down as hard as he could. Shiro gave one little cry and died.

*

□ それはいい。 Good idea.
□ 縄をつける tie a rope
□ 虫 bug
□ ひどい臭い terrible smell
□ 地団駄を踏む jump up and down

□ 〜を叱りつける shout at
□ 〜を手にとる pick up
□ 振りあげる lift

親切なおじいさんとおばあさんはそのことを知ると、とても悲しみました。二人とも泣きながら、死んでしまったシロを家につれて帰りました。そして、庭の角に、シロの墓をつくって、そこに埋葬したのです。そしてお墓のうえにちいさな松を植えたのです。

　すると何がおこったと思います？　なんと木が二人の目のまえで、どんどん大きくなるではありませんか。どんどん伸びて、家より高く、手を伸ばしても抱きかかえられないほど大きくなりました。

　「これはシロの贈りものじゃ」親切なおじいさんは言いました。「この木を使えば、これから死ぬまで料理をしたり、暖をとったりできる。幹を使えばきっとすばらしい臼ができる」

　「そうですね。臼をつくってくださいな、おじいさん」親切なおばあさんは言いました。「それでお餅をつくりましょう。シロがとても好きだったお餅を」

　そこで、おじいさんは木を倒して、幹から臼をつくりました。臼ができると、おじいさんはそれを台所にもってゆきます。おばあさんがお米を臼にいれて二人はそれぞれに杵を手にとります。

When the kind old man and woman found out about this, they were very sad. Both of them cried as they carried Shiro's body home. They dug a grave for him in one corner of their garden. Then they planted a little pine tree on top of the grave.

And what do you think happened next? The tree began to grow, right before their eyes. It grew and grew and grew, until it was taller than the house and too big to reach around.

"It's a present from Shiro!" the kind old man said. "With all this wood, we can cook and keep warm for the rest of our lives. And what a beautiful mortar the trunk will make!"

"Oh, yes! Please make a mortar, dear," said the kind old woman. "We can use it to prepare rice cakes. Shiro always loved rice cakes!"

So the old man cut the tree down and made a mortar out of the trunk. When it was ready, he brought it into the kitchen. The old woman put some rice in the bowl of the mortar, and they each picked up a mallet.

□ 墓をつくる→墓を掘る dig a grave
□ 埋葬する *bury*
□ 松 pine tree
□ 抱きかかえる reach around
□ 暖をとる keep warm

□ 幹 trunk
□ お餅 rice cake
□ 杵 mallet

「これはシロへの贈りもの」二人はそう言って、餅つきをはじめました。すると何がおこったと思います？　杵を持ち上げるたびに臼のお米が増えているのです。あっという間に、臼はお米でいっぱいに。それでもお米が湧いてきます。まもなく台所はお米でいっぱいになったのです。

「これはシロからの贈りものじゃ。これでわしらはずっと食べていける」親切なおばあさんは言いました。

*

お隣のいじわるばあさんはその話を聞くと、とても腹をたてました。いじわるじいさんも一緒です。

「なんであんな愚かな年よりばかりが良いめにあうのじゃ」じいさんは続けます。「あの臼をもらってくることにしよう」

じいさんは隣に行って臼を取りあげると、それを家に転がしてゆきました。そして台所において、いじわるばあさんがお米をそこに入れました。そして二人は杵を振りあげて、餅つきをはじめたのです。するとまもなく、臼は泥やゴミ、そして小さな虫たちでいっぱいになったのです。家中がひどい臭いに包まれます。

いじわるじいさんといじわるばあさんは、とても腹をたて、地団駄を踏んで怒鳴ります。そしてついにいじわるじいさんは斧をとって臼を切りきざみ、火のなかに放りこみました。

"This is for you, Shiro!" they said and began pounding the rice. And what do you think happened? Each time they lifted their mallets, they saw more rice in the mortar. In no time at all, the mortar was full, and still the rice kept coming. Soon the whole kitchen was filled with rice.

"It's a present from Shiro!" said the kind old woman. "Now we'll never be hungry again!"

*

When the mean old woman next door heard about this, she was very angry. Her husband was angry too.

"Why should those old fools have all the luck?" he said. "I'm going to borrow that mortar!"

And he marched right next door, turned the mortar over, and rolled it to his house. He set it up in the kitchen, and his wife put some rice in the bowl. Then they both picked up mallets and started pounding. And in no time at all, the mortar was full—of mud and waste and strange little bugs! A terrible smell filled the house.

The mean old couple were very angry. They jumped up and down and shouted, and finally the mean old man picked up his axe. He cut the mortar into little pieces and threw them in the fire.

□ 餅つき（をする）pound rice
□ （〜する）たびに each time
□ あっという間に in no time at all
□ 湧いてくる keep coming
□ 取りあげる turn over

□ 転がす roll
□ 斧 axe
□ 切りきざむ cut into little pieces
□ 放りこむ throw

親切なおじいさんが臼を返してもらいにくると、そこにはただ灰があるだけ。おじいさんは籠いっぱいに灰をいれると、悲しみながらそれを家に持って帰りました。

　「灰をシロの墓にまいてやりましょう」おばあさんはそう言いました。

　親切なおじいさんはおばあさんに賛成です。ところがおじいさんが外に出たときに、突然風が舞いました。そして灰を果物のなる木へと吹きとばしたのです。すると何がおこったと思います？

　それは真冬のことでした。木々はみんな枯れて枝だけになっています。そこに灰が降りかかると、なんといきなり木々は花でいっぱいです。

　「灰が花に様がわり」おばあさんはびっくりです。

　「これもシロの贈りもの」おじいさんも笑っています。

　おじいさんはとてもうれしくなって、少しばかり踊ります。籠を持って村に出て、灰を宙にまきながら歩いてゆきました。すると、スモモの木、桃の木、そして桜の木と、どれもが皆花ざかり。

　「私は花咲かじじい」おじいさんは叫びます。「枯れ木に花を咲かせましょう！」

When the kind old man came to get his mortar, nothing was left but ashes. He filled a basket with the ashes and sadly carried it home.

"We should leave the ashes on Shiro's grave, dear," said his wife.

The kind old man agreed. But when he stepped outside, a sudden wind came along. It blew some of the ashes on to the fruit trees. And what do you think happened next?

It was the middle of winter, and all the trees were dead and bare. But when the ashes landed on them, the trees were suddenly covered with flowers.

"The ashes turned to blossoms!" cried the kind old woman.

"It's another present from Shiro!" the old man laughed.

He was so happy that he did a little dance. Then he carried the basket out into the village. As he walked along, he threw ashes into the air. Plum trees, peach trees, and cherry trees flowered behind him.

"I'm Grandfather Flowers!" he cried. "My ashes turn to blossoms!"

□ 灰 ash
□ 真冬 the middle of winter
□ 枯れて枝だけになる be dead and bare
□ 降りかかる land on
□ 花でいっぱい be covered with flowers

□ 〜に様がわり turn to
□ 宙に into the air
□ スモモの木 plum tree
□ 花咲かじじい(じいさん) Grandfather Flowers

ちょうどそのとき、大殿さまが村を通りかかりました。大殿さまとその配下の人たちは長い旅をおえて、馬に乗ってお城に帰るところでした。

　「どうしたというのじゃ」大殿さまは、親切なおじいさんにききました。「何故そちは花咲かじじいと申しているのじゃ」

　「大殿さまに喜んでお見せ申しあげます」

　親切なおじいさんは、枯れた桜の木にのぼり、少し灰を撒きました。すると木はたちまち花でいっぱい。

Now, just at that time, a great lord happened to be passing through the village. He and his men were riding their horses back to the castle after a long trip.

"What is the meaning of this?" his lordship asked the kind old man. "Why do you call yourself Grandfather Flowers?"

"I'll gladly show you, your lordship."

The kind old man climbed a dead cherry tree. He threw some of the ashes into the air, and suddenly the tree was full of flowers.

□ ちょうどそのとき just at that time
□ 大殿さま great lord
□ 配下の人たち one's men
□ そち you
□ 〜と申す call (oneself)

「みごとじゃ！」大殿さまは叫びました。「この年よりに小判を授けよ」

　ちょうどそのとき、いじわるじいさんが走りより、親切なおじいさんから籠を取りあげると、

　「私めが、木を焼いて、この灰をつくりましたのじゃ！」と大きな声で言いました。「この金は私めのものでございます。私めが本当の花咲かじじいにございます。ご覧あれ」

　いじわるじいさんは枯れた桃の木にのぼって、残った灰をみんな撒きちらしました。ところが風が突然吹いたかと思うと、灰はまさに大殿さまの顔にかかります。

　大殿さまはとても怒りました。

　「この馬鹿ものを鎖につなげ！」大殿さまはそう命令します。

　いじわるじいさんは、お城につれていかれ、牢屋にいれられ、そこに長いあいだ閉じこめられていたということです。

"Wonderful!" cried his lordship. "Give this old man a bag of gold coins!"

Just then, the mean old man ran up. He took the basket from his neighbor.

"I burned the wood to make these ashes!" he shouted. "That gold belongs to me! I'm the real Grandfather Flowers! Just watch!"

The mean old man ran to a dead peach tree and threw all the ashes into the air. But a sudden wind came along and blew the ashes right in his lordship's face!

His lordship was very angry.

"Put this fool in chains!" he told his men.

They took the mean old man back to the castle and locked him in jail. And that's where he stayed for a very long time.

□ 走りよる run up
□ 〜のもの belong to
□ ご覧あれ。 Just watch.
□ 鎖につなぐ put in chains
□ 牢屋に in jail

A Straw Millionaire
わらしべ長者

昔々、ある村に一人の男が住んでいました。男はとてもいい人ですが、どうも運がありません。男は昼も夜も一生懸命働きますが、いつも貧しく不運なのです。

　ある日、男は観音さまにお参りに行きました。神さまどうか幸せになれますように。男は一日じゅう、飲まず食わずで、お祈りをしました。

　日が暮れて、あたりが暗くなってきたとき、観音さまが現れて申されます。「お前はここを離れるときに転んで、何かを見つけるであろう。お前はそれを手にして、西に行くがよい」

　男がそこを立ちさるとき、転んで何かを見つけます。それは藁でした。それは何の役にもたたないものですが、男はそれを持って西へと向かいます。

Long, long ago there was man living in a village. He was a good man, but he always had bad luck. He worked and worked from morning to night, but he was always poor and unlucky.

One day he prayed to *Kannon*, the Goddess of Mercy, for a happy future. He prayed all day, eating and drinking nothing at all.

When it became dark in the evening, Kannon appeared to him and said, "You are going to fall down and find something when you leave this place. You should take it with you and go west."

When he left the place, he fell down and found something. It was a straw. He thought it was useless, but he picked it up and carried it as he walked toward the west.

□ 運がない have bad luck
□ 昼も夜も from morning to night
□ 不運 unlucky
□ 観音さま the Goddess of Mercy
□ 〜にお参りに行く pray to

□ 飲まず食わずで eating and drinking nothing at all
□ 転ぶ fall down
□ 藁 straw
□ 何の役にもたたない useless

あぶが一匹飛んできます。男はそれを捕まえると、藁に結びつけ、再び歩きだしました。

　町にやってくると、赤ちゃんが藁に結ばれたあぶを見て泣きやみました。そのかわいい赤ちゃんに、男はその藁をあげました。お母さんはお礼にみかんを三つくださいました。

　男はみかんを持って、再び西へ歩きます。すると、道ばたに、若い女の人がいるではありませんか。女の人は喉がかわいていました。そこで男はみかんをあげると、やがて女の人は元気になります。お礼にと、女の人はきれいな絹の織物をくれたのです。

A horsefly flew to him. He caught it and tied it on the straw and started walking again.

When he arrived in a town, a baby stopped crying when it saw the horsefly on top of the straw. Seeing the happy baby, the man gave the straw to it. The mother thanked him and gave him three oranges.

He started walking west again, carrying the three oranges. He saw a young lady by the side of the road. She wanted water, so he gave her the oranges. Soon she felt better. To thank him, she gave him some beautiful silk cloth.

□ あぶ horsefly   □ 絹の織物 silk cloth
□ 泣きやむ stop crying
□ みかん orange
□ 道ばたに by the side of the road
□ 元気になる feel better

男はきれいな絹の織物を持って、また西へと歩きます。男はおさむらいさんと、病気の馬に出会いました。おさむらいは、きれいな織物を見ると、それと馬を交換してくれと頼みました。そしておさむらいは織物を持って東へと立ちさりました。男は病気の馬を一晩じゅう看病しました。すると、その翌朝、なんと馬は元気になったのです。

　男は再び馬をつれて西へと歩きます。お城のある町に着いたとき、お金持ちがその馬を見てとても気に入りました。男はお金持ちの家に招かれると、お金持ちの娘がお茶を持ってやってきます。驚いたことに、それはあのみかんを与えた娘だったのです。お金持ちは、この不思議な巡りあわせと、男のありがたい親切に、心を動かされます。そして、娘をこの男に嫁がせようと決心したのでした。

　男は、藁から富を手にいれました。観音さまの言うとおり。以来男はずっと、たとえ一本の藁でも大切にします。村の人は男のことをわらしべ長者と呼ぶようになったのでした。

He started walking west again with the beautiful silk cloth. He met a samurai and his sick horse. The samurai saw the beautiful cloth and ordered him to give it to him for the horse. The samurai took the cloth and went east. The man looked after the sick horse all night. The horse got well the next morning.

He started walking west again with the horse. When he arrived in a castle town, a rich man saw the horse and liked it very much. The man was invited to the rich man's house, where his daughter brought two cups of tea to them. To his surprise, it was the young lady that he had given the oranges to. The rich man was so moved at the strange meeting and at how kind the man was that he decided his daughter should marry the young man.

The young man became rich from the straw, as Kannon told him. He never forgot to take care of even one piece of straw for the rest of life. He was called *Wara Choja* (the straw millionaire) by the people in the village.

□ 一晩じゅう all night
□ 看病する look after
□ 招く invite
□ 不思議な巡りあわせ strange meeting
□ 心を動かされる be moved

□ 嫁がせる *marry (one's daughter) off*
□ 富 rich
□ ずっと for the rest of life
□ 長者 millionaire

Urashima Taro

うらしま た ろう
浦島太郎

昔々、あるところに浦島太郎という心やさしい漁師が住んでいました。ある日、海辺を歩いていると、浦島太郎は亀に出会います。村の子どもたちがいじめていたのを助けてあげたのです。

　数日の後、浦島太郎はいつものように、漁に出かけました。すると、あのとき助けた亀が、浦島太郎のところにやってくるではありませんか。

　「あのとき助けていただいた亀でございます。お姫さまが、竜宮城でお礼のおもてなしをしたいと申しております」亀はそう言いました。

　亀は、浦島太郎を甲羅のうえに乗せると、海にもぐって竜宮城につれていきました。

Long, long ago there lived a kind fisherman called Urashima Taro. One day, while walking along the beach, he saw a turtle. The village children were doing mean things to the turtle, but he saved it.

Several days later, he was fishing as always when the turtle he had helped came to him from the sea.

"I am the turtle that you saved the other day. A princess told me to bring you to the *Ryugujo* (Dragon Palace) to thank you," said the turtle.

It took him on its back to the Ryugujo under the sea.

□ 漁師 fisherman
□ 亀 turtle
□ いじめる do a mean thing
□ あのとき the other day
□ 竜宮城 Ryugujo (Dragon Palace)

□ おもてなし *hospitality*
□ 甲羅 *turtle's back*

竜宮城は、珊瑚がいっぱいの素晴らしいところでした。たくさんの魚がまわりを泳いでいます。しかも、浦島太郎は、乙姫さまというきれいなお姫さまに出会います。こんな美しい人ははじめてです。「浦島太郎さん。いつまでも、こころゆくまでおくつろぎください」

　乙姫さまはそう言いました。浦島太郎は、時の経つのも忘れ、夢のような日々を送ります。しかし、何年かして、浦島太郎は昔住んでいた村と、年老いた母親のことを思いだします。そろそろ帰らなければ。乙姫さまは、お別れに小さな箱をくださいました。そして言いました。

　「浦島太郎さん。これは玉手箱という魔法の箱。何か困ったことがあったとき、それを開けてくださいね」

　浦島太郎が亀の背に乗って村に帰ると、住んでいた家もなく、年老いた母もいません。村はとても変わってしまっていたのです。

　浦島太郎はどうしていいやらわかりません。そこで、あの小さな箱を開けたのです。すると煙が出てきて、浦島太郎は、瞬くまに、長く白いひげをはやしたおじいさんに変わってしまいました。

　海のしたで楽しく過ごしていたあいだに、この世では何百年も経っていたのです。浦島太郎は、いま自分がどこにいるのやら、これが夢かどうかすらわからなくなったということです。

The Ryugujo was a wonderful place filled with beautiful coral, and there were many fish swimming around in it. Even better, he met a beautiful princess named Otohime. He had never seen such a beautiful lady before.

"Mr. Urashima, please enjoy yourself here as long as you wish," said the princess.

He forgot the passing of time. Life there was like a dream. But after several years he remembered his old village and his old mother. It was time to go home. When she said goodbye to him, the princess gave him a little box as a present.

She said, "Mr. Urashima, this is a magic box called a *tamate-bako*. When you are in trouble, you can open it."

When he went back home on the turtle, he could not find his house and his old mother, and he found his village had changed a lot.

He did not know what to do. At last he opened the little box. When he opened it, white smoke came out of it, and he suddenly became an old man with a long white beard.

While he was having a happy time under the sea, hundreds of years had passed on Earth. He was not sure where he was now and did not know if it was a dream or not.

□ 珊瑚 coral
□ しかも even better
□ くつろぐ enjoy oneself
□ そろそろ〜(し)なければ it is time to do
□ お別れ(する) say goodbye

□ 困ったことがある be in trouble
□ 瞬くまに suddenly
□ ひげ beard
□ 何百年 hundreds of years

Issun Boshi

<ruby>一寸法師<rt>いっすんぼうし</rt></ruby>

昔々、なにわに若い夫婦が住んでいました。二人はいつも仲が
よく、皆から好かれていました。でも、二人には子どもがいませ
ん。そこである日、二人は住吉神社にお参りに行きました。

　「どうか子どもを授けたまえ」二人は神さまにそうお祈りをし
ました。「どんなに小さな子どもでも構いません、一人子どもを授
けたまえ」

　するとどうでしょう。数ヵ月ほどして、妻が小さな男の子を生
んだのです。それはとても小さな子どもでした。指ほどの大きさ
もありません。でもとても元気で生き生きとしていました。二人
は心からその子を大切にし、一寸法師と名づけたのでした。

　一寸法師とは、小さい子どもという意味です。やがて一寸法師
は5歳になりました。でも一寸法師の身長は変わりません。7歳
になっても、10歳になっても、そして12歳になっても。

　他の子と違うことは、子どもにとっては大変です。でも、他の
子がチビだといって笑うと、一寸法師も一緒になって笑うのです。
一寸法師は誰にでもいつもやさしく、にこにこしています。そう、
一寸法師の心はとても大きかったのです。

＊

Long, long ago in Naniwa, there lived a young man and his wife. They were both good people, and they loved each other very much. But, sadly, they had no children. One day they went to Sumiyoshi Shrine to pray.

"Won't you send us a child?" they asked the god of the shrine. "Just one little child of our own, no matter how small!"

And what do you think happened? Some months later, the lady gave birth to a little baby boy. A very little one, in fact. This baby was no bigger than your finger. But he was healthy and full of life, and his parents loved him with all their hearts. They named him Issun Boshi.

Issun Boshi means "Little One Inch." By the time he reached the age of five, Issun Boshi was still only an inch tall. The same was true at seven, and even at ten and twelve.

It wasn't easy being so different from other children. But when the others laughed at his size, Issun Boshi only laughed along with them. He was kind to all and always smiling. In other words, he had a very big heart.

□ 仲がよい love each other very much
□ 住吉神社 Sumiyoshi Shrine
□ どんなに〜でも no matter how
□ 数ヵ月ほどして some months later
□ 〜ほどの大きさもない no bigger than ...

□ 生き生きとしている be full of life
□ 心から大切にする love with all one's heart
□ チビ *shrimp*
□ （〜と）一緒になって along with

一寸法師は大きな夢を持っていました。ある日のこと、一寸法師はお父さんとお母さんのところに行って、深く頭をさげました。

　「父上、母上。私はこれから都に行きたいと思います」一寸法師はそう言いました。

　「京に行くとな。一人でかい」お母さんはそうたずねました。

　「はい。そこは日本で最もすばらしいところだと聞いています。そこで運を試してみたいのです」一寸法師はそう答えました。

　「しかし、お前はまだ子どもじゃないか」

　二人はかわいい我が子に旅に出てほしくはありません。しかし、とうとう二人は一寸法師に説得されてしまいました。

　「わかったぞ。息子よ」お父さんは言いました。「私たちは、お前には自分の望みをあきらめないようにと教えてきた。都に行って、立派な人になりなさい」

　「ありがとうございます。父上」

　一寸法師はすぐに旅じたくを整えます。お母さんは、大切にしていた縫い針を刀として一寸法師にわたすと、藁を帯に結びつけて、刀の鞘にしてあげました。そしてお父さんは、一寸法師のためにお椀を持ってきて、舟にして、お箸でお椀の舟を漕いでゆくようにしてあげました。

He also had big dreams. One day, Issun Boshi went to his parents and bowed deeply.

"Mother, Father," he said, "I want to go to the capital."

"To the City of Kyo?" said his mother. "All by yourself?"

"Yes," said Issun Boshi. "They say it's the most wonderful place in all Japan. I want to try my luck there."

"But you're so young…"

His parents didn't want their dear boy to go, but at last they agreed.

"Very well, son," his father said. "We always taught you to follow your heart. Go to the capital and become a great man."

"Thank you, Father!"

Issun Boshi was soon ready for his trip. His mother gave him her finest sewing needle to use as a sword, and she tied a straw to his belt to carry the sword in. His father gave him a soup bowl to use as a boat and a chopstick to use as an oar.

□ 都 capital
□ 一人で all by oneself
□ 運を試す try one's luck
□ 望みをあきらめない follow one's heart
□ 旅じたくを整える ready for trip

□ 縫い針 sewing needle
□ 鞘 *scabbard*
□ お箸 chopstick
□ 舟を漕ぐ *row a boat*

次の日の朝、皆で川まで歩いてゆくと、一寸法師はお椀の舟によじのぼり、それに乗ると、お箸で陸を押して川に出てゆきます。お父さんとお母さんは、手を振って別れを惜しむのでした。

「気をつけるんだよ。自分を信じてな！」

「母上、父上、おさらばです。必ず立派な人になって参ります」

少しずつ、くる日もくる日も一寸法師はお椀の舟をあやつって川をのぼってゆきました。時には強い風や大雨で、何度もお椀の舟はひっくりかえりそうになりました。そして何度も鳥や魚と闘わなければなりませんでした。でも、一寸法師はあきらめませんでした。

The next morning, they all walked down to the river together. Issun Boshi climbed into the soup bowl and pushed off with his chopstick. His mother and father waved goodbye.

"Good luck, son! Never stop believing in yourself!"

"Goodbye, Mother! Goodbye, Father! I'll become a great man, I promise!"

Little by little, day after day, Issun Boshi pushed his soup bowl boat up the river. He met with strong winds and hard rains. More than once his little boat almost turned over. And more than once he had to fight off birds and fish. But he never gave up.

□ よじのぼる climb
□ 手を振って別れを惜しむ wave goodbye
□ おさらばです。 Goodbye.
□ 少しずつ little by little
□ くる日もくる日も day after day

□ 何度も more than once
□ ひっくりかえる turn over
□ あきらめない never give up

そしてついに京についたとき、一寸法師は夢を見ているようでした。きれいな通りには人や馬や手押し車がたくさん。そして店々ではこの世にあるものはなんでも売っています。

「日本一の町だ」一寸法師は思いました。「皆が言っていたようにすごい町だ」

一寸法師は五条通りから三条通りへと歩いてゆきます。そこには、大きな家の門がありました。

「これはとても偉い人の家に違いない。ここで働けるか聞いてみよう」一寸法師は思いました。

一寸法師は、門からまっすぐ大きな玄関へと歩いてゆくと、そのすぐ前に立ち、大きな声で

「ごめんください！」と言いました。

三条の君はちょうど家にいたので、子どもの大きな声を聞いて玄関を開けましたが、そこには誰もおりません。

When at last he reached the City of Kyo, he thought he must be dreaming. The beautiful streets were filled with people and horses and carts, and the shops sold everything under the sun.

"The greatest city in Japan!" he thought. "It's just as wonderful as people say!"

He walked from Gojo, the fifth block, to Sanjo, the third. And there he came to the gate of a great big house.

"This must be the home of a very important man," he thought. "I'll ask if I can work for him!"

Issun Boshi marched right through the gate and all the way up to the big front entrance. He stood on the step and called out at the top of his voice:

"Excuse me!"

The Lord of Sanjo happened to be just inside the entrance. He heard the boy's shout and opened the door himself. But he couldn't see anyone.

□ 手押し車 cart
□ この世にあるものはなんでも everything under the sun
□ とても偉い人 very important man
□ 〜かどうか聞いてみる ask if

□ ごめんください。 Excuse me.
□ 三条の君 the Lord of Sanjo

「こちらです」一寸法師は叫びました。

なんと小さな子どもでしょう。三条の君はびっくり仰天。

「おまえは誰かえ」

「私はなにわの一寸法師と申します。立派な人になりたいんです。お殿さまにお仕えできますでしょうか」

三条の君は笑いだしました。とても面白そうな子に思えたのです。

「お前のような者をやとうとは。望むところじゃ」

一寸法師はすぐにこのお偉い方の一家の一員として迎えられました。しっかり働き、勉強し、いつも与えられた仕事は精いっぱいがんばりました。一寸法師は皆から好かれています。三条の君の娘でとてもきれいなお姫さまはとくに一寸法師を気にいっていました。一寸法師はこの世で一番かわいいと、お姫さまは思い、二人はすぐによい友だちになりました。

＊

"Down here, sir!" cried Issun Boshi.

Lord Sanjo was surprised to see such a small person.

"Who are you?" he said.

"I am Issun Boshi of Naniwa. I want to become a great man. May I work for you?"

Lord Sanjo laughed. He found this young man very interesting.

"I can use a man like you, Issun Boshi," he said. "Welcome!"

Issun Boshi soon became like a member of the great man's family. He worked and studied hard and always did his best at every job. Everyone liked him—especially Lord Sanjo's beautiful daughter, Ohime-sama. She thought Issun Boshi was the cutest thing in the world, and they soon became the best of friends.

*

□ 〜にお仕えする work for
□ 精いっぱい do one's best
□ よい友だちになる become the best of
　friends

夏が過ぎ、秋が来たかと思えば、もう冬です。そして春のある日、お姫さまは清水寺に桜を見にいきたいと言いました。若い男たちや女たちが一緒にお姫さまと花見に行きます。一寸法師も一緒でした。

　お寺に向かって森を歩いてゆくと、薮のなかで音がします。突然大きな青鬼が一行のまえに立ちはだかりました。鬼は馬ほど大きく、目は真っ赤、そして歯は長く尖っています。けたたましい音を出しながら、お姫さまのところにやってくるではありませんか。お姫さまは気を失って倒れてしまいました。

　他の男も女も皆一目散に逃げてゆきます。でも一寸法師だけは畏れませんでした。一寸法師は鬼とお姫さまのあいだに立って、あの針の刀を引きぬきます。

　「こちらは三条の君のお姫さまであるぞ。すぐに立ちされ、さもなければお前を打ちのめしてやる」

　鬼は笑いました。

　「なんだと。お前は朝飯のおかずにもならぬなあ！」鬼はそう言うと二本の指で一寸法師をつまみあげました。そして、高く持ちあげたかと思うと、自分の口の中に放りこみます。

Summer passed, and then autumn and winter. One day in spring, Ohime-sama said she wanted to see the cherry blossoms at Kiyomizu Temple. A group of young men and women agreed to go with her, and Issun Boshi joined them.

They were all walking through the forest on the way to the temple, when they heard a noise in the brush. Suddenly a big blue demon jumped out in front of them. This demon was the size of a horse and had red eyes and long, pointed teeth. It made a terrible noise and reached for Ohime-sama. She fell to the ground in a faint.

The other young men and women all turned and ran away at once. Issun Boshi alone was not afraid. He stood his ground, between the demon and Ohime-sama, and pulled out his needle sword.

"This lady is the daughter of Lord Sanjo!" he shouted. "Leave her alone, or I'll cut you down!"

The demon laughed.

"Why, you're not even big enough to make a good breakfast!" it said. It reached down and caught Issun Boshi between two fingers. Then it lifted him high in the air and dropped him into its mouth.

□ 清水寺 Kiyomizu Temple
□ 一行 *party*
□ 尖っている pointed
□ けたたましい音 terrible noise

□ 気を失って倒れる fall to the ground in a faint
□ 一目散に逃げる turn and run away at once

気がつくと、一寸法師は、長くて暗いトンネルのなかにいます。でも一寸法師はひるみません。刀の切っ先を、トンネルのやわらかい壁に突きさします。そしてそれを抜くとまた突きさします。

　「俺さまのなかで、これは痛い！」鬼は叫んでころがりまわります。「やめろ！　降参だ！」

＊

　一寸法師は、鬼の口から飛びでると、鬼の足に針を突きたてました。鬼は泣きながら一目散に逃げてゆきます。

　お姫さまはそのときすでに気がついていました。

　「私はすべてを見ていました。私の命の恩人ね」お姫さまはとおしそうに一寸法師を見つめています。

　「とんでもございません」一寸法師は言いました。

　「あなたはすてきな方。おや、見てごらんなさい」

　お姫さまはそう言うと、地面にころがった奇妙な木づちを指さしました。

　「これはなんでしょう」一寸法師が不思議に思うと、

　「鬼が残した魔法の木づちですよ」とお姫さまが言うのです。「あなたの望みはなんでもかなえられるのです！　おっしゃってください。私の大事な人」

Issun Boshi found himself in a long, dark tunnel. But even now he wasn't afraid. He pushed the point of his sword into the soft wall of the tunnel. Then he pulled it out, and then he pushed it back in.

"My insides! They hurt!" the demon shouted and danced about. "Stop! You win!"

*

Issun Boshi jumped back out of the demon's mouth and drove his needle into its foot. The demon cried and ran for its life.

Ohime-sama was awake now.

"I saw everything!" she said and looked at Issun Boshi with the light of love in her eyes. "My hero!"

"Oh, it was nothing," he said.

"You were wonderful!" she said. "But look!"

She pointed at a strange hammer on the ground.

"What is it?" said Issun Boshi.

"The demon dropped his magic hammer!" she said. "Any wish you make with this will come true! What do you wish for, my hero?"

□ 気がつくと〜にいる find oneself in ...
□ ひるむ be afraid
□ 刀の切っ先 point of a sword
□ 一目散に逃げる run for one's life
□ 気がついて awake

□ いとおしそうに with the light of love in one's eyes
□ とんでもございません。 It was nothing.
□ 木づち hammer

一寸法師は、木づちに手をおくと目を閉じました。そして目を開けると、一寸法師は大きくなっていたのです。

　お姫さまは口を大きく開けてびっくり仰天。

　「一寸法師。あなたはとても背が高くてすてきな人」

　一寸法師の名は都に知れわたり、都で出世します。そしてお姫さまと結ばれて、大きな家に二人で越してゆきました。やがて二人はなにわに行って、一寸法師のお父さんとお母さんを都につれてもどりました。

　そして幾ひさしく幸せに暮らしましたとさ。

Issun Boshi put his hand on the hammer and closed his eyes. When he opened them again, he was fully grown.

Ohime-sama's mouth fell open.

"Oh, Issun Boshi!," she said. "You're so tall! And so nice looking!"

Soon Issun Boshi was a famous and important man in the capital. He and Ohime-sama married and moved into a big house of their own. In time, they traveled to Naniwa and brought his parents back with them.

And they all lived happily ever after.

□ 口を大きく開けて mouth fall open
□ 出世する be an important man
□ やがて in time
□ 幾ひさしく幸せに暮らす live happily ever after

The Golden Boy

きん た ろう
金太郎

昔々のこと、足柄山という山に、金太郎という男の子がお母さんといっしょに住んでいました。金太郎のお父さんは、おさむらいで京都に住んでいましたが、戦で死んでしまったのです。

　お母さんは、戦を避けるために、山の奥深くへ金太郎をつれてゆきました。「どんなことをしてでも、この子を夫のように立派なさむらいに育てなければ」お母さんはそのように自分に言いきかせていました。

　二人は洞窟のなかに住んでいたので、誰も見つけることができません。食べるものがなかったので、お母さんは金太郎のために果物や木の実、野いちごなどを摘んでいました。

　お母さんは、昔はとてもきれいでした。でも、今ではそんな美貌もすたれてしまっています。お母さんのきれいな着物も汚れてやぶれてしまいました。二人は貧しいけど、お母さんは金太郎を大切に思い、いつもたくさんの食べ物を金太郎のために用意していました。

Long, long ago, on a mountain called Mt. Ashigara, there lived a young boy called *Kintaro* (the Golden Boy) and his mother. His father had been a samurai in Kyoto, but he was killed in a war.

His mother, who ran away from the fighting, brought Kintaro deep into the mountains. "I must make my son a great samurai like my husband any way I can," she said to herself.

The two lived in a cave so no one would find them. She picked fruit, nuts and berries for him because they did not have any other food.

At one time, she had been very beautiful, but now she lost her beauty. Her beautiful clothes became dirty and worn out. They were poor, but she loved Kintaro and gave him a lot of food.

□ 足柄山 Mt. Ashigara
□ 戦で死ぬ be killed in a war
□ 山の奥深く deep into the mountains
□ どんなことをしてでも any way one can
□ 言いきかせる say to oneself

□ 洞窟 cave
□ 野いちご berry
□ 美貌 beauty

やがて、金太郎は元気いっぱいの楽しい子どもに育ちました。
毎日、金太郎は山に住む多くの動物たちと相撲をとって、次から
次へと動物たちを投げとばしていました。

　「くまさん。君の番だ、かかってこい！」金太郎はそう言うと、
金太郎と同じぐらい強い大きなくまと戦います。長い取りくみの
のち、金太郎はくまを投げたのでした。

　相撲のあと、金太郎は動物たちと森に走ってゆきました。そし
て、猿からは木ののぼりかた、鹿からは森のなかでの走りかたを
学びます。

　友だちの一人に川に住む大きな鯉がいました。金太郎は、その
鯉が水からはねて飛びでたとき、助けてあげたのです。金太郎は
早瀬のなかを鯉が泳ぐとき、背に乗って遊びます。

Soon he grew up to be a cheerful boy with a lot of energy. Every day he did sumo with the many animals living on the mountain. He threw one animal after another.

"Dear Bear, it's your turn. Come on!" he said, and fought with the big bear, which was just as strong as he was. After a long match, he threw it.

After the fight, he ran in the forest with the animals. He was taught how to climb trees by a monkey and how to run in the woods by a deer.

One of his friends was a big carp living in a river. He had saved the fish when it jumped out of the water. He enjoyed riding on the carp as it swam up the fast-moving river.

□ 元気いっぱいの with a lot of energy
□ 楽しい cheerful
□ 次から次へと one after another
□ 君の番だ。 It's your turn.
□ 取りくみ match

□ 鯉 carp
□ 早瀬 fast-moving river

雨が降ると、金太郎は一日中動物たちと洞窟にいます。ねずみやりす、狐、あなぐま、猿、うさぎ、くま、それにもっと他の動物たちにも食べものを与えるのです。ですから金太郎は動物たちの人気者です。

　そんな金太郎を見て、お母さんは、神さまにお祈りをします。「金太郎はきっと立派なさむらいになります！」

　何年かが過ぎて、春がやってきました。ある日金太郎は、動物たちと隣の山に旅に出ました。

　金太郎は大きなくまのうえに乗って、まさかりを担いで、猿やりす、そしてあらいぐまに狐、そして猪や鹿をつれてゆきます。皆で楽しく旅をしました。

　崖までくると、したに流れの速い川があるではありませんか。「川の流れが速すぎて、わたれないぞ」金太郎は言いました。

　「僕が大きな木を押したおして、橋をつくるよ」くまは言いました。でも、木はとてもがっしりしています。

　猪が木にむかって走ってきて、頭をぶつけますが、葉っぱが動いただけでした。

When it was raining, he spent all day with the animals in a cave. He gave food to mice, squirrels, foxes, badgers, monkeys, rabbits, bears and other animals. He was very popular among them.

Looking at her son, his mother prayed to God, "May he be a great samurai!"

Several years passed, and spring came. One day, he went on a trip to the next mountain with the animals.

He sat on a big bear, carrying his hatchet on his shoulder, and with him were a mouse, a squirrel, a monkey, a rabbit, a raccoon, a fox, a boar and a deer. They really enjoyed the trip.

Reaching a cliff, they found a big river moving fast under them.

"The river is so fast that we can't cross it," said Kintaro.

"I will push down a big tree and make a bridge," said the bear, but the tree was too strong.

The boar ran at the tree and hit it with his head, but only the leaves moved.

□ 一日中 all day
□ あなぐま badger
□ 人気者だ be very popular
□ まさかり hatchet
□ 担ぐ carry something on one's shoulder

□ 猪 boar
□ 崖 cliff
□ がっしりした strong

「よし、僕がやってみよう」金太郎はそう言うと、木の前に立って何度もそれを押しました。

動物たちはびっくり。木が動いて、ついに大きな音とともに倒れたではありませんか。そしてやっと崖をわたれる橋ができたのです。

みんなとてもうれしくなりました。そのとき、誰かがうしろで話しかけています。「なんと力のある子なのじゃ」そこには一人のさむらいが、配下をつれて立っていました。

「わしの名は 源 頼光じゃ。わしの家来になってはくれぬか」

「おさむらいになれるのですか」金太郎はびっくりしてそう言いました。

「間違いなく、わしの家来のなかでも最も立派なさむらいになれるじゃろう」

金太郎はお母さんのいる洞窟にもどると、「私は父上のような立派なさむらいになって参ります」と言いました。お母さんはうれしくて目に涙を浮かべます。しかし、金太郎と別れることは寂しいかぎりです。

"OK, I will try," said Kintaro, and he stood in front of the tree. He pushed and pushed.

To the animals' surprise, the tree moved and then fell with a big noise, making a bridge between the two cliffs.

Everyone felt very happy. Then somebody spoke to them from behind. The voice said, "What a powerful boy you are!" A samurai and his men were standing there.

"My name is Minamoto-No-Yorimitsu. Why don't you join me?"

"Can I be a samurai?" asked Kintaro with surprise.

"I am sure you'll be one of my greatest samurai," said Yorimitsu.

He returned to the cave where his mother lived and said to her, "I will be a great samurai like my father." She was so happy that tears came to her eyes, but she was sad to say goodbye to him.

□ びっくりして with surprise
□ 家来 *retainer*
□ 間違いなく〜だろう。 I am sure ...
□ 目に涙を浮かべる tears come to one's
   eyes

山を去るとき、動物たちもお母さんも悲しそうに金太郎を見おくりました。

「今まで仲よくしてくれてありがとう。絶対みんなのことは忘れないよ。そして大好きなお母さん。きっと帰って参りますから」金太郎は何度も手を振りながらそう言いました。

何年かして、金太郎は立派なおさむらいになって、坂田金時と名のります。京都では、金太郎は頼光の四天王のひとりに数えられ、大江山に住む鬼たちも退治しました。

金太郎は、お母さんを京都に招き、末ながく幸せに暮らしたということです。

When he left the mountain, the animals and his mother saw him off with sad faces.

"Thank you for being my friends. I will never forget you. I love you, Mom. I am sure I will return home in the future," said Kintaro, waving his hands again and again.

A few years later he became a great samurai named Saka-ta-No-Kintoki. In Kyoto, he was chosen as one of the four most important of Yorimitsu's men and killed demons living on a mountain called Mt. Oe.

He invited his mother to Kyoto, and they lived together happily ever after.

□ 見おくる see off
□ 何度も again and again
□ 四天王 the four most important
□ 大江山 Mt. Oe

本書は2011年に弊社から刊行された『対訳ニッポン双書 日本昔ばなし』(カルラ・ヴァレンタイン訳)を元に再構成したものです。

装幀・カバー写真＝斉藤　啓(ブッダプロダクションズ)
本文イラスト＝菊地玲奈

Furigana JAPAN
日本昔ばなし
Long-ago Stories of Japan

2021年4月3日　第1刷発行

訳　者　カルラ・ヴァレンタイン 他

発行者　浦　晋亮

発行所　IBCパブリッシング株式会社
　　　　〒162-0804 東京都新宿区中里町29番3号 菱秀神楽坂ビル9F
　　　　Tel. 03-3513-4511　Fax. 03-3513-4512
　　　　www.ibcpub.co.jp

印刷所　株式会社シナノパブリッシングプレス

© IBC Publishing, Inc. 2021

Printed in Japan

ISBN978-4-7946-0656-3